EDUCATING ANDY

Educating Andy

The Experiences of a Foreign
Family in the Japanese
Elementary School System

Anne and Andy Conduit

KODANSHA INTERNATIONAL
Tokyo · New York · London

Distributed in the United States by Kodansha America, Inc., 114 Fifth Avenue, New York N.Y. 10011, and in the United Kingdom and continental Europe by Kodansha Europe Ltd., 95 Aldwych, London WC2B 4JF. Published by Kodansha International Ltd., 17-14 Otowa 1-chome, Bunkyo-ku, Tokyo 112, and Kodansha America, Inc.

ISBN 4-7700-1921-1

CONTENTS

Preface

For those working in intercultural relations in the business sector in Japan, literature abounds on both the theoretical and practical aspects of working with Japanese people, and particularly, of working in a Japanese company. The focus of most of that literature is the rigid set of operating skills expected in the Japanese work environment; the intricacy and efficacy of this environment is no longer astounding when one experiences their initial implementation in the Japanese primary-school system.

In essence, what the Japanese corporation requires of its newly hired graduates are a sound academic preparation and a well-defined set of particular skills for operating in Japanese society. Since employment opportunities are frequently linked to the university from which one graduates, and universities in Japan are hierarchically ranked according to the caliber of their students, under the Japanese education system the objective of each student's academic experience is to pass the university entrance examinations with the highest possible score—if he or she aspires to continue studies at the tertiary level. Traditionally, therefore, education up to the end of high school has been extremely rigid and demanding, followed (for those who go on to higher education) by a period of comparative relaxation and enjoyment at the university where the student has won a place. University students are not prepared in their studies for specific occupations (with the exceptions of science and medicine), but follow rather more generalized studies that build on the sound academic base

7

they have acquired prior to entering the university. Companies, which hire most new recruits directly from the universities, then mold the new employees through substantial training in their corporate culture. However, the training is predicated upon new employees possessing a sound academic preparation and the particular values for operating in Japanese society, both of which are the focus of education from primary school onward.

From 1991 to 1994, my son, Andy, and I had the opportunity to appreciate the crucial links between what is learned in the Japanese primary school and what is required in the *kaisha* (corporation) while participating in the Japanese primary-school community. This book describes some of our experiences and impressions.

* * *

For the wonderful experience with the Honmura primary school, and the possibility of this book, we are indebted to many. First and foremost we would like to thank the headmaster and teachers for going out of their way to make our association a pleasant one. To all the friends we made among parents and pupils we would also say a warm thank-you.

For the many interesting episodes associated with the activities of the Honmura Baseball Club, we are grateful to coaches, parents and team members who made us feel so welcome.

We would also like to thank Andy's Kumon and violin teachers during our stay in Japan and others in the community surrounding the school.

Finally, we are indebted to relatives and friends for their encouragement and support as we wrote about our experiences.

PROLOGUE

I was called up onto the stage. The principal said something like, "This is Andy Conduit. He will be entering fourth grade, first section," and then he asked if I wanted to say anything, but I said, "No thank you quietly to him." Now that I have been at the school for two years, I realize what I should have done is say, "*Yoroshiku onegaishimasu*" and made a short speech introducing myself.

On the day I went to my new Japanese primary school, my mother and I went into the principal's room. He said something like, "Welcome to the school. If you wait five minutes I'll call the teacher of fourth grade, section one." Then the teacher came in, and Mum and the teacher talked a bit, and then the teacher, half-joking, turned to me and said, "Oh, you're very tall! We'll need a big desk for you." After the teacher had talked to us she went up to the classroom, but we were asked to wait in the principal's room until 8:30. Then we went to the gymnasium, where they were having their Monday all-school meeting. On the stage in the gymnasium, I felt very embarrassed because I'd never stood up in front of a whole school before, and when I looked down at the crowd, the whole school was staring up at me.

After the morning meeting had finished, at about 8:45,

9

I was put in the line for fourth grade, section one, and we went out of the gymnasium. We had to march, and I thought this was very childish because I'd never marched out of a school assembly before, even when I was little. We had to march like soldiers and I thought it was really a bit babyish at the time. I felt very uncomfortable, but now I just take it for granted and do it.

After leaving the gymnasium, you can split up out of your "soldier" marching line, and when we did that, as we were going up the stairs, they kept asking me, "How many centimeters tall are you? How much do you weigh? Have you ever seen a koala bear?" or weird questions like that. I thought, "Why are they treating me like an alien?" Then in the classroom they were kind of chitterchattering about me and Australia, and the teacher came in, so we stopped and we had a class morning meeting. I'd never had one of these. Because everybody had been chatting so much before, the teacher had a little question time, and they all asked me questions like "Have you ever seen a kangaroo?" I remember I was trying to learn everybody's names. I think I only got about four people's names right at first, but one memory is that there was a guy, and because I'd learned about four guys' names before him—enough for me!—I couldn't take in his name. He was wearing a Popeye tank top, so I called him "Popeye."

ANNE'S STORY

I was finally in a position to empathize with mothers of migrant children in Australia. There I was, sitting in the principal's office, discussing through an interpreter my son's future education in the school with the principal and his class teacher. None of my studies in language and culture, my training as an ESOL (English to Speakers of Other Languages) teacher, or my experience living and working in foreign countries could have prepared me for the sensation of complete helplessness I felt at that time. I was virtually powerless to guide the situation in any way— at the mercy of those in control. The only difference between me and the migrant mother, at that moment, was that for me there were other options.

INTRODUCTION

THE ORIGINS OF THIS BOOK

Collection of information for this book began quite coincidentally. I was a little worried, when Andy went into the Japanese primary school full-time as a fifth-grader, that his English would suffer. Furthermore, he from time to time encountered situations that really bothered him and needed talking through, or writing about. I thus encouraged him to keep a diary of events on the computer. He was never terribly diligent about it, but this diary later formed the nucleus for this text.

At that time, in 1992, there was a concentrated focus on Japan's economic success as well as much research in the area of comparative education, particularly between Japan and the United States. Many renowned scholars had spent a lot of time observing the Japanese system from *yōchien* (kindergarten) to *daigaku* (university), but from my own reading of their materials, I felt that it might be interesting to view the same system through the eyes of a child experiencing it, particularly if that child were old enough to make valid comparisons and had had enough experience in other systems for a comparison to matter. Friends and family expressed interest in Andy's experiences, and it was suggested that something more serious should be made of it in writing. At the time, however, I was inundated with my university work and had no way of keeping up a record, or of pressing Andy to write up his experiences. I therefore began to use a tape recorder to interview Andy about aspects which I found interesting from an intercultural point of view. Much of the narrative part of the text is based on those recordings.

WHY A JAPANESE SCHOOL?

Our family of three had moved to Japan in December 1989 as a result of my husband's posting to Tokyo with Austrade, the Australian Trade Commission. I too had been very fortunate to have been able to pursue my own career path, having obtained a teaching position in a Japanese university in Tokyo on the basis of my work and studies at the University of Sydney. Our son, Andy, was eight years old.

Prior to our departure, Austrade made a post report available to us. This was a regularly updated information package which gave a general background on the country of assignment, covering as many aspects as possible, from the purely informational such as political and economic briefings, history, language, and customs, to more practical aspects of daily life, such as where to shop and what education options were open for children and spouses. Schools suggested for the children were international schools which followed an American or British-based curriculum, or schools of particular ethnic allegiance such as the French School or the German School.

I had wondered for some years, on previous postings abroad, why the local schools in the host country were rarely, if ever, considered as options by Australian diplomats; and with Australia's strong political and economic commitment to becoming part of Asia, I felt that local schooling would surely be a way to introduce our son to the linguistic and cultural experience available in Japan.

However, like most government service employees, we initially chose an international school, opting for the one which seemed to offer the best Japanese-language program among the schools available. The school was the closest approximation to a bilingual/bicultural school in Tokyo at the time. In reality, however, due to the transient expatriate population, it proved to be bilingual/bicultural for the Japanese children, but not for the expatriates. The school offered two different programs for learning Japanese: one for native speakers and those children who had one Japanese parent, and a separate one for expatriate children. Andy's Japanese language program enabled him to study Japanese for one hour each day, largely focusing on reading and writing. Through the program he was able to participate in various cultural activities offered by the school to enhance intercultural understanding. No matter how much Japanese language studies were encouraged, and despite the fact that 50 percent of the students in the school were native speakers of Japanese, natural segregation of expatriates from the Japanese occurred; the expatriate children experienced very little interaction using the Japanese language. The Japanese language program thus became our first area of concern.

The international school followed an American-based curriculum, and many of the values underlying the system did not seem to suit Andy. For example, in his former schools, Andy had become used to a very competitive system with explicit rewards for excellence, in which there had been a strong concentration on basic preparation, particularly in English grammar and mathematics. The international system we encountered was not as competitive, and in the third grade was already focusing on writing academic-style papers complete with bibliographies as well as on intricate problem-solving math, even though many of the children were not able to analyze the structure of an English sentence, spell, or do fairly basic calculations.

Combined with all this, the international system had the children on vacation from the first week in June until the beginning of September—nearly three months—with additional holidays at Christmas and Easter, for a total amount of approximately four months per year. Expatriate lifestyle in Tokyo did not easily accommodate leisure activities for children, and such long holidays seemed both endless and counterproductive. The international schools did provide a three-week summer school program in June, but our impression was that it was more like a holiday camp than a pedagogical environment. All in all, the American system in a Japanese environment did not meet Andy's needs at that time.

At the same time, my own interest in the Japanese school system was increasing. While Andy was experiencing his first school in Japan, I was deeply involved with my teaching assignment, which I was finding professionally gratifying and stimulating. The university at which I was teaching is highly regarded among the hierarchically ranked Japanese tertiary institutions, and my students were some of the most interesting of my teaching career. I had taught in many "English to Speakers of Other Languages" situations—in Canada, Italy, Libya, Indonesia, and Australia—but the Japanese experience was the most challenging and stimulating I had encountered. In the first place, students were highly motivated, self-disciplined, and with an organizational capacity for learning which I much admired. It seemed to me that, despite criticism for lack of self-expression and lateral thinking skills put forward by many Western teachers, basic Japanese education had not only achieved an extremely high level of literacy, but also inculcated in the students a set of basic learning skills which, with a little direction, were a delight for a dedicated teacher of English and intercultural communication.

About 90 percent of the students came to their first-year university classes with a loathing for English language studies, a result of the rigid studies directed toward the university entrance exam. Those studies were almost entirely based on rote memorization, and the concept of learning itself was almost always associated with stress, endurance, and hard work. However, on the positive side, the reading ability and knowledge of grammar in the English language achieved through these studies provided a strong foundation from which to introduce some more exciting communicative language activities in order to focus on language as a communication tool rather than purely as an academic discipline. Once the students came to enjoy their studies, a more lateral and deductive thinking process could gradually be encouraged through small research projects and other learning activities specifically chosen for the intercultural sensitivity level of the group.

My own academic training had been rather unusual in that I had moved from undergraduate studies in business and commerce to postgraduate studies in applied linguistics. As part of a master's program, I had studied a sociological view of language and intercultural communication, and my research interests were immediately directed toward the relationship between language and culture. I was teaching two courses in intercultural communication skills at the university, one specifically on intercultural communication skills, the other on introducing the sociological view of language to analyze spoken language. The first course covered general concepts involved in intercultural communication: cultural self-awareness, values across cultures in specific areas such as the family, education and the company, a study of language and non-verbal behavior in a message, and differences in perception. The second course focused on the ways in which culture influences the message. I felt that it was important, particularly for the intercultural communication skills course, that the academic environment should benefit from what actually happened in intercultural situations and vice versa. So I approached one of the larger trading companies in Tokyo to see if I might become involved in some of the training programs in intercultural communication which had become very much part of corporate training in both Japan and the United States. I was invited by the company to conduct the biannual, intercultural communication training course at head office. From the outset, it was apparent to me in my work there that the values demanded by Japanese society in the corporate world were extremely marked, and strongly influential in intercultural communication problems. I hypothesized that, since the objectives of the Japanese education system were to prepare individuals to take their eventual place in the business world, perhaps this preparation actually began as early as the primary school.

As so often happens in life, a combination of circumstances—in this case place, time, dissatisfaction with current schooling, interest in Andy's acquisition of Japanese language, admiration for certain values found in Japanese university students, curiosity about the origin of underlying values in the Japanese *kaisha* (company), and Andy's positive attitude—led us to a Japanese primary school experience for Andy.

ANDY'S EXPERIENCE WITH OTHER LANGUAGES AND SCHOOLS

Andy began his life in an environment responsive to several languages and has continued to benefit from similar environments. He was born in Milan in 1981, and lived there until he was two. At that time, my husband held a senior Australian government position in northern Italy. Although his primary role was the promotion of trade between Australia and Italy, he was also required to represent the Australian government in that region on other matters as requested. The job was a busy and interesting one, in which I was required to play a supportive role. Since much of my time was taken up in these duties, a full-time nanny was employed to take care of Andy. We were fortunate to find a remarkable Filipina woman, who adored the child and was particularly patient in teaching him both English and some of her native language, Tagalog. Since I had spent some ten years in Italy prior to marriage, I enjoyed speaking Italian and interacting with the Italian people. As a result, Andy was very comfortable in his language environment of Italian, English, and Tagalog.

From Milan we moved to Indonesia, where Andy entered an Indonesian kindergarten and spoke Bahasa Indonesia quite comfortably at home with the household help and at the kindergarten. Ten years later, his only recollection of that kindergarten was as follows:

> *All I remember about the kindergarten in Jakarta was that we all had to paint a picture as soon as we arrived, before the Indonesian teachers would let us play on the swings. I preferred to play! They were very kind to us, though—I've heard Mum say they were a bit too kind at times!*

At four, he entered the British School in Jakarta and spent a year there. The British School offered strong guidelines with rigid implementation of basic skills, which seemed to suit his personality well. In one year he had learned most of his basic mathematical tables and could read reasonably well. His memories of that school are short:

> *At the British School we used to win emblems when we did well at anything and these had to be sewn on to our uniforms. We really liked those emblems.*

We then returned to Sydney, and Andy spent the first year in a state school there, which turned out to be somewhat dissatisfying for both academic and social reasons. The British School in Jakarta had the children reading early, and the particular state school we chose for him in Sydney had rigid age-based guidelines as to what material children should be reading at any time. Although Andy could already read, he was not allowed to do so at that school. In addition, he was much younger than the other children in his class and found socializing difficult. We therefore moved him, for the last two years of our stay in Sydney, to an excellent private school with a system very like that of the British School he had attended in Jakarta, and he was very comfortable there until we moved to Japan. By that time, Andy was quite used to changing schools and languages, so the idea of trying a Japanese school did not worry him at all.

First Encounters

EASING INTO THE SYSTEM

Part-time

We arrived in Tokyo in December 1989, and Andy entered the international school immediately after Christmas, in January 1990. His nose was put slightly out of joint when, having excelled in his Australian third-grade end-of-year exams in December, he was then told he had to do a further six months in third grade in the international school until June, since it followed the American academic year. The academic years of Australia, Japan, and the United States do not synchronize, as illustrated in figure 1.

The Australian academic year runs from late January/ early February to early or mid December, with school holidays four times each year—about two weeks in March/April, three weeks in June/July, two weeks in September/October, and seven weeks in December/January.

Figure 1. Academic Years of Australia, Japan, and the U.S.

Key
Australia _____
Japan   _ _ _ _ _
U.S.A.   ....

Jan Feb Mar Apr. May Jun. Jul. Aug. Sep. Oct. Nov. Dec

!_____!

_ _ _ _ _ _ _ _ _ _!   !_ _ _ _ _ _ _ _ _ _ _ _ _ _ _ _ _ _

...................................!   !...

The Japanese academic year runs from April to the end of
March, with six weeks holiday in July/August, two weeks
in December/January, and two weeks in March/April. The
American academic year runs from September to June,
with two weeks holiday in December/January, two weeks
holiday in March/April, and eleven weeks holiday in
June/July/August.

Andy still remembers his experience at the international school fondly. He made friends with other expatriate children from all over the world, and shared the
learning environment with the Japanese children who
comprised half of the student population.

When the international school year finished in June of
1990, my husband and I enrolled Andy in the three-week
summer program organized by his international school.
We were not impressed. Furthermore, when he began
fourth grade the following September, his main complaint
was that the work was boring: the pupils spent the first
few weeks reviewing what they had done in third grade to
refresh their memories after such a long summer vacation.

With the Japanese language program in the international school focused on perfecting reading and writing skills—following the Japanese Ministry of Education guidelines—we became rather concerned that Andy's learning experience was not equipping him to take advantage of the opportunities available for communicating with Japanese people using their language. We were lucky that year to find a Japanese woman who came to the house once a week to teach Andy and a friend speech and drama in Japanese, which they loved. She had them prepare their own dramas, writing the parts in Japanese (with her help) and then practicing and performing them.

Early in 1991, with the prospect of another long summer holiday looming ahead and the frustration of finding expatriate children seemingly unable to take advantage of the Japanese environment for learning the language, I decided to find out whether it would be possible to have Andy accepted as a guest in a local Japanese school. I had calculated that the timing might fit rather well, since the international school finished in early June and the Japanese school did not finish until about July 20. If it were possible to arrange, this would leave approximately six weeks for the experience.

Of course, I had no idea how to go about carrying out this plan. However, at the international school there was a much-respected senior Japanese teacher who had been one of the founding teachers of the school and was a strong supporter both of international education and of education for global awareness. I approached her with my idea and asked her for suggestions. She had worked closely with the principals of a number of Japanese primary schools in the area, and suggested that one in particular might be receptive. In the meantime, I found out that by law one is supposed to enroll children in the primary school closest to the family residence. I therefore visited the Japanese primary school across the road from the Australian Embassy compound where we were living at the time, and found that it would be possible to enroll Andy there; in fact, the school already had almost a dozen foreign children, none of whom were from English-speaking backgrounds. There were Chinese and Korean children, and several from eastern European countries.

Encouraged by the results of my first approach, I then arranged an interview with the headmaster of the school recommended by the senior Japanese teacher. I prepared my questions beforehand, and took an interpreter from the Embassy with me on the first occasion. The principal was very welcoming and invited Andy to join the school as a summer guest in the same grade he was currently finishing at the international school (grade 4), which later proved appropriate for his level of Japanese language. For no other reason than that I felt more comfortable having the support of the international school, I decided to take up this second option rather than approach the new experience in the Japanese primary school closest to our residence as a total stranger. Once the decision was made, I then went to the ward office without an interpreter and filled out the form required to enter school.[1] It was certainly not the first time that a child had been accepted as a guest in the Japanese system, but the experience was still relatively rare, and to be negotiated on a case-by-case basis.

The initial encounter with the Japanese primary school was somewhat daunting for Andy. However, we spent considerable time talking it through with him; we told him that he needn't stay on if, after one week's trial, he really hated the experience for any reason. Fortunately, we never had to use this escape clause. From day one, Andy loved the Japanese primary school, finding his social encounters with both teachers and students a challenge yet thriving on the learning experiences to which he was being exposed. When summer holidays began for the Japanese children and school was out, we discussed the experience with the Japanese principal and teachers, and all agreed it had been positive. This encouraged me to ask the principal if it might not be possible for Andy to rejoin his Japanese classmates on Saturdays from September, while continuing in fifth grade at the international school.[2] We were fortunate to have encountered a principal who was positive about intercultural experience, and Andy was allowed to continue in both schools beginning in September of 1991, attending the international one from Monday to Friday and the Japanese one on Saturdays.

During the summer holidays we encouraged Andy to take a positive attitude toward Japan by taking advantage of some of the many opportunities for intercultural exchange available in Japan. One of these is the Chichibu festival[3] held in Saitama prefecture, about three hours by bus northwest of Tokyo. In this area the local people host seventy foreign children from as many different nationalities as possible for four days, during the town's festival period at the end of July. Children are taken from Tokyo by bus and are placed in a homestay with a Japanese family. The children participate in all the festival cultural activities such as processions and parties, as well as specially arranged activities in sports and Japanese crafts. Andy spent a delightful four days in Chichibu in 1991 with a family who had hosted a boy from Pakistan the year before.

The YMCAs in Japan organize holiday camps during all school holidays. In 1991 Andy participated in one of these with two Japanese friends from the international school. While the overall experience was positive, there were certain adjustments that had to be made, as indicated in the text of a note I found among his belongings upon his return from the camp:

> *I absolutely hate being big and strong. I also hate not being able to understand what everyone's saying. Also everyone's teasing me when the leaders aren't there. I don't know if I should tell or not. If I tell I am a dobber but, how can I just let them do this to me? For an example of not understanding—they were throwing Alexander's hat around and the second time I got it back to him (after I saw him hitting people). He then said they weren't teasing him.*

Andy is a big child for his age; he had obviously felt his size among the Japanese children. Alexander was one of the friends who had accompanied him from the international school. Alexander's mother is Japanese and his father American, so he was probably in better control of the situation than Andy was. Andy obviously couldn't understand enough to know quite what was going on and intervened on Alexander's behalf when he thought the other children were keeping Alexander's hat from him, with Alexander then not the least bit grateful. Andy sadly took himself off into a corner and wrote about it to get it out of his system.

Full-time

Andy's dad was transferred to Singapore unexpectedly in late January 1992. There was no doubt in our minds that Andy should attend junior high school (Australian high

Andy with host family in Chichibu.

Andy at festival.

school) in Australia. However, in 1992 he still had two more years of primary school to complete, and another new school would have been his seventh. I was still very stimulated in my working environment, so after much family discussion it was decided that I would remain in Tokyo with Andy, and that he and I would commute to Singapore to spend the school holidays with his father.

Andy finished the 1991/92 American academic year in the pattern of Monday to Friday at the international school, and Saturday at the Japanese school. By this time he was completely at home in the Japanese system. Furthermore, I could not afford the US$15,000 (¥1,500,000, A$19,700)[4] school fees required at the international school. It was thus decided that Andy would finish primary school full-time in the Japanese system.[5]

The bureaucratic transition from part-time to full-time status was very smooth, because any foreign child holding an alien registration card is entitled to attend Japanese school on a full-time basis. Part-time enrollment is more difficult because a child cannot legally be enrolled in two schools at the same time; it is entirely up to the principal whether or not to accept a child on a guest basis. In June 1992, Andy had completed fifth grade in the international school, and he continued in fifth grade at the Japanese primary school until March 1993. Then, at the beginning of the Japanese school year in April 1993, he began sixth grade, which he almost completed before returning to Australia in late January 1994.

Joining the Neighborhood

The lifestyle Andy and I followed while we were involved full-time with the Japanese primary school was markedly different from a Western one. First of all, we moved into Japanese-style accommodations outside the embassy compound. This involved learning the rituals associated with renting, becoming accustomed to a residence about one-tenth the size we had been used to, and learning to use this new situation to experience a Japanese, rather than an Australian, lifestyle in Japan. This all proved to be a great deal more comfortable than I had imagined.

Because schools are zoned in Japan, and because you are supposed to attend the primary school in your neighborhood, we were obliged to stay in the same ward as the embassy—one of the most expensive areas in Tokyo—to avoid changing schools yet again. We were most fortunate in almost immediately finding a suitable place at a reasonable price. The real estate agent and the owner of our apartment were not at all reluctant to rent to foreigners, a complaint often heard in Japan. We were rather shocked when we had to advance ¥1,000,000 (A$13,000, US$10,000) to get into the place—one month's rent plus two months' rent as refundable deposit, one month's worth of rent as gift money to the owner, and one month's worth to the agent. (We actually paid less than the norm, having negotiated to pay only one month's non-refundable gift money to the owner, instead of the more usual two.) Of course, as is required for both housing and jobs in Japan, a guarantor who would vouch for us while we were in Japan had to be sought. I found approaching Japanese for this very humiliating, but not as humiliating as being fingerprinted for the new "alien registration" documents of identification that I needed after leaving the embassy!

We moved into two rooms—one six-tatami-mat room and one twelve-mat room[6]—plus kitchen and bathroom.

By Japanese standards in the price range—¥200,000 per month (about A$2,600, US$2,000 at the time)—our accommodation was well appointed: it had built-in cupboards, wall-to-wall carpet, kitchen cupboards, a stove with four gas rings, and a Western-style bath. The two rooms were separated by the kitchen and bathroom, allowing Andy to consider one room his, and me to stay up later in the "living room" without disturbing his sleep.

Once we moved out of the embassy we embraced our new Japanese lifestyle with enthusiasm. Operating in a small space is part of that lifestyle—thus futons[7] on the floor for bedding, only essential furniture and possessions, and shopping every day or two for food. This lifestyle proved extremely conducive to keeping fit—our only means of transport besides walking being bicycles. I had worried about how I would keep Andy entertained in such a small space, but this proved to be no problem, since many activities were organized by the school on the school grounds. Indeed, the new situation proved easier in some ways than the expatriate one had been: for example, Andy no longer had to be driven to after-school activities. Everything centered around the school or within the area; members of the community all knew each other, alleviating the risk of danger to children. That I was effectively a single parent caused no concern, since Japanese parents often separate for educational purposes. To ensure that their children hold their place in the Japanese education system, Japanese mothers usually stay with the children while the fathers complete their work assignments overseas or elsewhere in Japan.

My timetable at the University was very accommodating. Teaching months were from April to July and from October to January; I finished my last class at 3:00 in the afternoon and was able to be home not long after Andy. On occasions when I was delayed, he always had plenty to do with homework, extra Japanese, and violin practice, and was thus fully occupied. He also learned much about household management over that period, both from school and through doing the shopping, simple cooking, and message-taking in my absence. During the months when I wasn't teaching, I was writing academic papers or preparing courses, both of which could be done at home.

It was nevertheless a very busy time when I had teaching commitments—a constant juggling of shopping, cooking, cleaning, laundry, and profession. One of the most difficult things, above all that, was my own illiteracy in the Japanese language. Of course I was continually studying Japanese (as I still am), but the difficulty of the language is such that it takes many years for an adult to become literate at the rate I was studying—on average three hours per week during teaching months and one hour per day otherwise. I was very lucky to meet a supportive group of mothers from the school early in our experience. A few of them had lived abroad, and they were most willing to give me the gist of the memorandums from school over the phone in the evenings, or telephone me if there was any urgent communication that they thought I might miss. All in all, I don't think we missed out on too much!

THE JAPANESE PRIMARY SCHOOL

Facilities

The facilities at the Japanese primary school could not be faulted; they provided for the needs of every child in the school, including the handicapped. The Honmura primary school had been completely rebuilt and the new facilities inaugurated in June 1992. There had been a primary school on that same site since 1903, and in 1993 we joined many present and past pupils in celebrating its ninetieth anniversary. We were all given special souvenir books on that occasion showing pictures of the school and its staff and pupils in various eras.

For a school in the center of Tokyo, where space is at a premium and land prices are some of the highest in the world, Honmura occupied an extremely large area and was very well equipped.

The school had a very large playground at the rear, which could be conveniently converted to a one hundred-meter oval running track, tennis courts, one soccer field, or two dodge-ball courts. This area was also used for school assemblies on fine days. On one side of the playground was a small lake which contained tadpoles in the summer and some tiny fish. Near this lake was a chicken and rabbit house, a sandpit, and a jungle gym. Three school flagpoles, on which the Japanese flag, the Minato-ward flag, and the school flag were flown, were located in front of the chicken house. On the other side of the sports area were the class gardens, each approximately two meters by one meter, in which the children grew vegetables or flowers, usually for science projects. (For example, they might grow corn, study it, then cook it and eat it. Sometimes they grew flowers and conducted pollen tests.)

Entering the school from the playground at the rear, one encountered the nurse's room, the handicapped children's classroom, and the principal's office, along with a very large room where all the teachers worked together

Honmura primary school
at time of founding.

New school building.

outside class time, at individual desks—the usual layout for the adult work environment in Japan.

Teacher's work room.

Children's dining room.

Science lab.

Library.

Classroom.

Swimming pool.

Gymnasium.

There was also a large dining room, where lunches were served, on the basement level.

On the ground floor, one floor up, was the entrance from the street, a reception area, two computer rooms, a multipurpose room, and classrooms for grades 1 and 2. The studio for school intercom and TV transmission was also located on this floor, as were the music rooms.

On the second floor were two fourth-grade classrooms, two third-grade classrooms, the home studies room, the science laboratory, the art room, and the library.

The third floor housed two fifth-grade classrooms and two sixth-grade classrooms.

There were two additional basement areas: in the lower one were two changing rooms and the gymnasium, and in the higher, two changing rooms and the twenty-five-meter heated swimming pool.

School Organization

Japanese children have traditionally attended school six days a week, with Sunday the only rest day. However, in the 1992/93 school year, every second Saturday of the month was designated a rest day, in a move toward eventually implementing a five-day school week. The school hours were also reduced slightly during the month of July because of the heat.

For timetable purposes, the school was divided into "age cohorts" depending on the activity—sometimes three (grades 1 and 2, 3 and 4, 5 and 6), but more often two: the higher grades 4, 5, and 6, known as *kōgakunen*, and the lower grades 1, 2, and 3, called *teigakunen*. The higher grades had a slightly longer school day than the lower grades: the lower were dismissed at 2:00 P.M. on Mondays,

THE JAPANESE PRIMARY SCHOOL 37

Tuesdays, Thursdays, and Fridays, while the higher grades stayed on until 3:45. All classes were let out at about 2:00 on Wednesdays and about 12:00 on Saturdays.

The school gates did not open in the mornings until 8:15, but some children would meet in front of the gates to play as early as 7:30. There was great emphasis on punctuality, and punishments could be harsh for late arrivals, depending on the teacher. There was always a teacher on duty at the school entrance responsible for meting out punishment. Generally speaking, if a child arrived after 8:25 this was considered late and written down in the class notebook by the teacher on entrance duty, to be seen by the class teacher later. A child arriving after 8:30 was considered exceptionally late and would be reprimanded by the class teacher. If the child was habitually late, the class teacher would become very angry. The time from 8:30 to 8:45 was generally dedicated to meetings of various kinds; in addition to special meetings, there was always a class meeting to start the day, and also one to finish the day. Morning recess was from 10:20 to 10:40, and hot lunch was served at 12:15. On Mondays, Tuesdays, Thursdays, and Fridays, twenty minutes of playtime was allowed after lunch, before the period allotted to school cleaning.

As in most schools, a school diary was given to parents at the beginning of the academic year in April. This indicated school holidays and public holidays as well as important dates for the year. It was quite important for parents to know when hot lunches would begin being served and when they stopped; at the beginning and end of terms there were one or two days for organizing the kitchens; on those days it was expected that children would return home for lunch, which marked the end of their school day. Since Japan is located in an earthquake zone, fire and earthquake drills were often held in the primary school. Parents were expected to be involved and pick up their children at the appropriate place and time afterwards. Dates for excursions and sports meetings, as well as for parents to visit the school or attend parent-teacher interviews, were also communicated. Excursions to museums, factories, or parks were held several times each year for each grade. A school sports meet was held in May, an inter-school sports meet in October, a swimming meet in September, and a concert at some stage during the year.

Chapter 2

The Program

THE CURRICULUM

A nationally identical curriculum is followed by all schools in the Japanese system, including Japanese international schools abroad. With the entire education system geared toward the rigid university entrance exam at the end of high school, a national curriculum is imperative. On one of our commutes to Singapore when Andy was in Grade 5, we were very intrigued to see some Japanese fifth-grade students going home from school on our bus, carrying the same textbooks Andy was using in Tokyo and handmade backpacks just like the one he had finished making the week before in the home studies class.

Andy's timetable for sixth grade (see figure 2) gives a good indication of the range of subjects and activities offered.

Figure 2. Sixth Grade Timetable 1993/94

Time	Monday	Tuesday	Wednesday
8:15–8:25			ENTER
8:30	General Assembly (weekly aim) Morning Meeting	Morning Meeting	Sports/Music Morning Meeting
8:45–9:30	Japanese	Math	Art
9:35–10:20	Calligraphy	Japanese	Art
			RECESS
10:40–11:25	Social Studies	Science	Music
11:30–12:15	Social Studies	Science	Math
			LUNCH TIME
12:55	RECESS	RECESS	Closing Meeting
1:15	Cleaning	Cleaning	Class Reps. Meeting
1:35	Class Group Time	Social Studies	
2:00			
2:20			
2:35	Closing Meeting	Physical Education	
3:05	Club		
3:20		Closing Meeting	
Dismissal	3:45	3:45	2:00

Thursday	Friday	Saturday
School Groups Morning Meeting	Morning Meeting	Teacher Communication Morning Meeting
Math	Physical Education	Japanese
Japanese	Japanese	Math
Home Studies	Math	Everybody's Time
Home Studies	Music	Closing Meeting
RECESS	RECESS	
Cleaning	Cleaning	
Physical Education	Science	
Ethics	Closing Meeting	
Closing Meeting		
3:45	2:35	11:50

The subjects in the Japanese primary school curriculum consisted of Japanese Language, Calligraphy, Social Studies, Math, Science, Physical Education, Art, Music, Home Studies, and Ethics. In the upper grades, the periods per week dedicated to each of these were as follows:

Japanese	5	Physical Education	3
Calligraphy	1	Art	2
Social Studies	3	Music	2
Math	5	Home Studies	2
Science	3	Ethics	1

Andy described his learning experiences in each of these subjects to me:

Q: Tell me about Japanese.

A: Sometimes we'll read a story out of the textbook and study towards that story on different things. Sometimes [we think of] how to make a picture in your mind. We think of the characters in the story—what they are thinking. One thing that we always do is study *kanji* [Chinese characters] from the stories. Some are *kanji* that we have studied before, with different ways of reading, and some are new.

Q: What do you do in calligraphy class?

A: We usually spend two periods on one *kanji*. Occasionally we practice with a pencil. Usually the teacher gives us a *kanji* and she'll explain on this special board where you put water on the brush and write and it appears black. It disappears after a while. She'll explain and then we'll write. We're all supposed to know the stroke order, but she explains the angle of the brush, or how to turn the corner, or how to *haneru*—when you stop and then flick to make like a hook. Then we go up to the front and get three pieces of paper, usually three, and we write. Sometimes we go to the teacher and ask her to look at what's wrong with the *kanji*, then after three or more papers, if you're satisfied, you go up to the teacher with what you think are the two best papers. First she asks which you think is the best, and then she says which she thinks is the best. Then she asks which you think is the best after hearing her opinion. Then, by the second time on the same letter, she's marked the papers with a red brush, to show you if you're turning your brush the wrong way; she'll write on top of it if it is wrong in red. So she gives that back to you, and you can see what you have to change. Then, after seeing the marked paper, you write a final copy. That gets stuck up at the back of the room.

Q: Why does it get stuck at the back of the room?

A: I think for the class teacher to see or something. It's like in international school—just to put up your work.

Q: And do you like calligraphy?

A: Yep ... except for one thing. It gets on your clothes so you can't wear your favorite clothes to school on a Monday [calligraphy day].

Q: What about social studies? Do you have a textbook for that?

A: Yes, we have a textbook for everything.

Q: What have you been learning about in social studies?

A: Well, in sixth grade we've been studying history. In fifth grade we studied about the community, rice paddies, farming, and stuff. But lately we've been studying about a guy called Nobunaga who ... becomes the leader of the country, and then that guy gets killed and then somebody else becomes the leader. One person is a guy called Ieyasu, Tokugawa Ieyasu. Well, his family stayed the leader of Japan for about 260–80 years. When you think of the Japanese learning way, you think, memory, memory, memory, but it's not really like that. The teacher doesn't make us learn all the dates and everything. We've just got to learn a couple of dates—when somebody's killed and when it changes and why it happened. That's about all that we have to learn about dates.

Q: Do you find that social studies program interesting?

A: Yes. At first I thought it was a bit too much about your own country, because we didn't study anything about any other countries. It's only Japan. I'd studied about the other countries in the other school, but I wanted to keep on doing that.

Q: What do you do in math class?

A: Well, it's divided into chapters of the textbook. When we start a new chapter we don't use the textbook at first. The teacher will explain it, then we'll look in the book at the rules and stuff. Then we'll do the problems in the textbook. If we're in the middle of a chapter, we'll just go straight into doing different type of work under the same heading or continue the problem solving. If it's division of fractions, say one third and one half, you only have to multiply the bottom. Then, the next time, the teacher will show us top and bottom. The next time she'll show us how to reduce the fractions and then multiply.

Q: How does she introduce a new chapter?

A: Well, she has different ways according to the contents

of the chapter. Sometimes she'll just go right in and say we're going to study this, this and this, and this is how you do it. One time we were doing one versus two and she used making caramel as an example, and actually made it for us. Other times she'll just start writing and then ask what kind of a mathematical name we think something would have.

Q: Is it interesting?

A: Yes, very.

Q: How does it compare with your other [the international] school?

A: Well, at the other school there was such a long summer vacation we had to spend the first month or two repeating, so it was boring.

Q: What about science?

A: Science is good. There are lots of experiments and stuff. In one we used a gas burner—there are special gas outlets in the science laboratory, and we hooked them all up—and wrapped a wooden chopstick in aluminium foil so no air could come in and we made it so the flame was in the middle of the wrapped chopstick. We put the fire of the gas burner on the aluminum foil and lit a match to the end of the chopstick, and after a while the foil started to crinkle. When we took the match and gas burner away from the chopstick, the chopstick just kept on burning like a gas burner for a while. We learned that even if there's no air some *moeru kitai* [flammable gas] comes out.

Q: What about physical education?

A: Aren't you going to ask me if there's a textbook for that?

Q: Of course not. There's no physical education text-book.

A: Yes, there is. It explains.... When we're doing soccer it'll explain the rules, or if it's aerobics, how to do it. There is a textbook.

Q: So what kinds of things do you do ... all kinds of sporting things?

A: Yes. The ones I hate, though, are the bar where you have to do gymnastics. Also, I hate doing the handstands because I've never done them before and I'm hopeless at them. I'm too big.

Q: Do you participate then?

A: Yep. But I couldn't do them. You have to put your hands down, stand up, and roll or something. At first, of course, you can't just do it like that, and so the teacher has to hold you up; and the teacher was scared to hold me, because I was, you know, too big.

Q: What about art?

A: Art ... well, actually, we get into trouble for it because everybody's talking while they're doing the work so the teacher gets mad.

Q: Do you have a textbook for art?

A: Yep.

Q: What's in it?

A: Well, good hints and stuff and pictures of other people's work. Say we're doing a model clay person: there'll be pictures of other kids' model clay people to see how they're done, and you can learn from it ... like, "Oh I'm not going to do mine like this." It's very helpful.

Q: And how does the art program compare with the international school art program?

A: For some reason I began to like art. I used to hate it
      when I was in the international school although I
      began to like it a bit at the end. I am beginning to
      like it now—not that I'm going to be an artist though.

Q: What do you do in music?

A: Well, that's also where the teacher's getting mad be-
      cause it's noisy.

Q: That's not your class teacher?

A: No, the music teacher's not our class teacher. Al-
      though our class teacher is quite a good singer. Some-
      times we'll do a group thing; that's what we're doing
      now. Sometimes you're given a piece and sometimes
      we choose it, but usually we choose out of the text-
      book or there's a primary school songbook. It's got
      about three hundred pages and it's got all sorts of
      songs in it.

Q: And how can you choose it, if you don't know how it
      sounds?

A: We do know how it sounds. We're in sixth grade so
      we've studied most of them. We choose a song, and
      decide who's playing what, and in this case I'm play-
      ing the violin.

Q: How many instruments can you choose from?

A: Whatever's in the music room, except for the trum-
      pets, because they're too noisy. There are all sorts of
      xylophones. Some are like a piano so you stand up
      with your stick and go tong, tong, tong, and there's a
      foot pedal at the bottom that you can push down
      like the one on the piano that makes the notes long.
      And there's a new one that the school's just bought.
      It's got a rotating thing and a switch so you can make
      it slow or fast, and when you put your foot down and

you've turned the rotating thing on, it'll make vi-
brato at that speed.

Q: You've learned many instruments at that school.
How many have you learned?

A: The recorder, the trumpet, the *kemban* harmonica—
that's a piano you blow air into, the organ—just a
simple one like a piano that you pump air into, the
xylophone, the drums, and the keyboard.

The music program must be the best I have encountered in any of the schools that Andy has attended. All
children learn to read music very early in the primary
school, and everyone is encouraged to participate in learning songs and playing instruments. In fact, the first school
event we attended was a school concert in July of 1991,
when Andy had only been at the school for three weeks as
a summer guest. What impressed me most was that every
child in every class had some sort of part in the performance; they had even set aside a small part for Andy,
knowing he would be there on the day. The simplicity and
effectiveness of the costumes was also quite remarkable.
The children made their own costumes in class from crepe
paper, garbage bags, and anything else available.

Q: What goes on in the home studies program?

A: Well, lots of things. In sixth grade we make an apron
or a cover of some sort like a pillow case. In fifth
grade we made a backpack. You order them from a
company that fits the regulations. They give you the
material and the threader for the bag, and you have
to sew the material up into the shape of the bag and
everything, and you have to do the tacking by hand—

long stitches to keep it in place so you can machine sew over it.

Q: Do you only do sewing in home studies?

A: No. We cook! We've cooked egg and bacon, and *miso shiru* [Japanese soup]. We did rice, which is very difficult if you do it the old way. These days you just put it in the rice cooker and turn on the switch. Before, you had to swish it around, let it sit for thirty minutes, cook for ten minutes on low, ten minutes on medium, ten minutes on high, leave it for ten minutes and then you could finally serve it.

Q: Wow. That's pretty *taihen* [difficult], isn't it?

A: Yes. We do pancakes and lots of things as well.

Q: And do you eat them after you cook them?

A: Of course.

Q: Anything else in this home studies program?

A: Oh yes. There's how to keep a diary of your pocket money, how to keep your desk clean, and that kind of stuff.

Q: What about things at home?

A: We did ironing once, and washing.

In addition to the curriculum subjects set down for each class, there were school activities.

Q: On Wednesday, there are sports and music before the morning meeting?

A: Not "*and* music." The school is divided into the *kōgakunen* and *teigakunen*. We swap so we have one group doing the sports meeting and the other doing music. In music you just sing and stuff like that. The music is in the gym and the sports outside. The sports program changes every month, so sometimes

we do running, sometimes we do skipping rope, or
sometimes exercises.

Q: Then you go up to the classroom and have the morning meeting?

A: Yes.

EXTRACURRICULAR ACTIVITIES

Cram Schools

While the basic academic preparation in the primary
school was, in our experience, good, it was not sufficient
to prepare the Japanese children for the rigid entrance
tests for the private junior high schools to which many of
them aspired. Nine years—six of primary school and three
of junior high school—constitute the free and required
school education in the Japanese system. An extensive system of private and public three-year high schools lies beyond; virtually all students today go on to high school,
but admission to high schools is not automatic, and is
mediated by competitive examinations. Seventh graders
are entitled to enroll in their neighborhood public junior
high schools, but increasing numbers of them are opting
to enter private junior high schools that give children a
head start in the winnowing process that high school entrance involves. At Andy's school, many of the families
made concentrated efforts to have their children enter private junior high schools.

The fees for a private school per child on average were
¥500,000 (approximately A$6,580 or US$5,000) per year.
The entrance exam itself for each school cost ¥25,000
(A$330, US$250). One could take as many entrance tests as
one chose. Academic preparation for these tests usually

began in fourth or fifth grade, but could began as early as kindergarten, when the students began attending cram schools (*juku*), some of which were themselves ranked and had their own entrance tests.

One friend's child, a girl in sixth grade, attended *juku* on Tuesday, Wednesday, Friday and Saturday from 5:30 to 8:50 P.M. and on Sunday all day from 8:30 A.M. to 3:10 P.M. The cost of this was ¥27,000 (A$355, US$270) per month plus ¥3,000 (A$40, US$30) per month for testing. Subjects studied in this *juku* were math, Japanese, science, and social studies; the lessons consisted mainly of <u>rote learning</u>, with some analytical problems in math. Not all *juku* students chose four subjects. Some only took two, usually Japanese and math. The choice depended on the type of junior high school they aspired to enter. Our friend's daughter took four subjects, and was given *juku* homework in math on a regular basis and very little in the other three subjects. Another friend's son, also in sixth grade, attended *juku* on Tuesdays and Thursdays from 5:00 to 9:00 P.M., on Saturdays from 3:00 to 8:30 P.M., and all day Sunday for testing. His fees were ¥46,350 (A$610, US$463) per month. A third friend had her son attending *juku* on Tuesdays, Thursdays, and Fridays from 5:00 P.M. to 9:00 P.M., and Sundays all day for tests. The cost was ¥30,000 per month, but in addition they were paying ¥3,000 per hour for extra tutoring on Mondays and Wednesdays for two hours each time and on Saturdays for five hours (a total of ¥27,000 (A$355, US$270) per month). That boy was asthmatic, and his attacks increased as exam time drew near, so his parents finally withdrew him from the *juku* but continued with the tutoring.

Since regular school finished between 3:30 and 4:00 P.M.

and the *juku* lessons often began at 5:00 or 5:30, the children would have a snack after school and their dinner after *juku*, or sometimes they took a *bento* (box meal) with them to the *juku*. As soon as school was out for summer holidays—around July 20—the sixth graders began *juku* full-time, and their mothers launched into the a daily ritual of delivering fresh *bento* to the *juku* at midday and again in the evening. When asked how they felt about this, the mothers all said they felt it was part of the system and that it was their duty as mothers to encourage it. Furthermore, they insisted that their children enjoyed the classes at *juku* more than those at regular school, since the *juku* ones were more interesting.

Because Andy was in the primary school to improve his Japanese and appreciate the Japanese way of doing things, and would be returning to Australia for high school, we elected not to send him to a cram school which prepared the children for junior high school. However, there is a more basic type of cram school called Kumon, which offers math, Japanese, and English and is now available in some Western countries—Australia, the United States, and the United Kingdom among them. According to many Japanese mothers, their children used this system when younger to acquire basic mathematics skills and *kanji* reinforcement, or in higher grades to keep up with the mathematics, Japanese, or English in the school curriculum. The Kumon program was used in Tokyo by some foreigners, particularly those who wanted their children to progress in Japanese and those who felt that then children had a lack of rote-learned mathematical skills. Andy had been attending since his first days at the international school for math and Japanese language skills, and continued to do so after he entered the Japanese primary school. He had daily homework to do, and twice a week he attended the local Kumon classroom (these are located in many neighborhoods, and run on a franchise basis by trained instructors) where he had his homework corrected and was given his new assigments. His time at Kumon averaged an hour and a half each visit, and his homework took approximately one hour per day for the two subjects. However, in the later stages of his stay in Tokyo, the homework time increased to about two hours per day. When asked if he liked going to Kumon at the time, his answer was always that he didn't particularly like it, but it was just something everyone did. His recollections after the event, however, are somewhat different:

> We were all crowded into a very small room where we had to sit on the tatami floor round knee-high tables to do our study. Kids laughed and joked and threw things like erasers round the room or at each other. The toilet was almost part of the room and had the most annoying flush in the world.

I have been told that Toru Kumon, the founder of Kumon, and Shinichi Suzuki (of violin fame) were old friends from their academic years. Interestingly, both men based their learning methods on rote memorization, and both methods have succeeded in permeating Western countries. Certainly, the rote memorization skills which Andy learned in these two systems facilitated his learning then, and have continued to do so. They seem to be associated with the photographic memory skills required for learning so many kanji in the Japanese language, which in turn enable learners to recall other factual information and knowledge very quickly.

Recreation

With all the emphasis on academic preparation, I was interested to find out exactly how much time was spent in study, and how much recreation time, if any, students had. I decided to pass out a very simple form, asking parents at the school to classify their child's activities over one week. I wrote to the school to ask for the principal's permission to hand out the forms in class, but unfortunately I was told this kind of research was not permissible for a private individual. Through my own network of contacts in the school, I distributed about eighty forms privately, forty-six of which were returned. The age distribution of children for whom responses were received is shown in figure 3.

Figure 3. Distribution of Responses Showing Children's Activities						
Grade	1	2	3	4	5	6
Boys	2	5	1	2	3	10
Girls	2	4	3	4	3	7
Total	4	9	4	6	6	17

It is obvious that such a small sample will not produce statistically relevant information. However, my objective for this book was not to write an academic treatise, but rather to paint a picture of the patterns in one small group in Japanese society.

The hours children actually attended school were slightly fewer in grades 1, 2, and 3 than in grades 4, 5, and 6. Distribution of the children's time over their various activities is shown in figure 4. Children's bedtimes in the younger grades tended to be around 9:30 to 9:45, while in the higher grades it was usually around 10:30. Children in the younger grades tended to sleep an average of 9.3 hours per day, compared to 8.8 in the higher. A social studies survey the children did at school revealed that the children in Andy's class slept an average of 6 hours per night, but my research showed a little over 9 hours per night in first grade, decreasing to approximately 8.5 by sixth grade.

Figure 4. Weekly Distribution of Time in Hours

Grades	1		2		3		4		5		6	
Sex	Boys	Girls	Boys	Girls	Boys	Girls	Boys	Girls	Boys	Girls	Boys	Girls
Study	2.5	2	2.5	2.5	12	6.8	13.5	5.7	3.6	6.3	12.05	10.42
Cram	0	0	0	4	0	0	6.3	5	6.3	8.8	4.8	11.2
Play	36.5	31	30.4	40.8	34	29.6	19.2	30	28.6	33	31.95	17.25

Precise instructions on categorization of activities were not given with the form. Study time is therefore likely to include both homework from school and homework from cram school, and shows a marked increase in grade 6, as would be expected with many of the children preparing for the junior high entrance exams. However, there were those who elected to adhere to the system rigidly and studied a lot, and those who scarcely studied at all; among the boys in sixth grade, for example, there was one boy whose parent marked 27 hours of study, and one boy whose parent marked 0. Andy also remarked that some children did not do the school homework at all; some of them studied only for cram school, and others did no studying at all.

The pattern of figures for cram school shows an overall increase in hours with age, as expected, with a high average in the fourth grade boys of 6.25 hours (due particularly to one boy's 13.5 hours), and a low of 4.8 for the sixth grade boys (as some parents probably included "cram school" in "study," while some boys at this stage opted to devote their whole lives to baseball and computer games, doing no *juku* study and rarely any homework). I noted some children doing as many as 27 hours of cram school, many children doing 6–8 hours, and some doing none at all. Some parents steered their children away from the exam-oriented system at the primary school level, preferring their children to take up more serious study later, in either junior high school or in high school.

Play or recreation time figures are surprisingly high, but one must keep in mind that these included TV and computer games, which seemed to be the rage all over the globe at the time. Whereas the girls decreased their "play" time in sixth grade, boys apparently did not. But, as mentioned before, more of the boys seemed to opt out of the rigid exam system than did the girls. I found this behavioral pattern particularly interesting in light of the fact that possible career paths for women are still quite restricted in Japan.

The most popular extra-curricular activities besides *juku* were piano, swimming, and baseball; typically Japanese skills such as calligraphy and *soroban* (abacus) are also studied. Andy was a member of the baseball team and also studied the violin under the Suzuki method.

Chapter 3

Socialization—
The Individual

RESPONSIBILITY FOR PERSONAL HEALTH, HYGIENE, AND APPEARANCE

Considerable care was given to the physical well-being of the children and included instruction on how they could take care of their own health. Children were encouraged to be spotlessly clean, pay attention to their health, and present a well-groomed appearance.

Medical Care

The school had a nurse who was a permanent member of the staff. Some of the children acted as her assistants for group activities and learned how to administer first aid to other children. Each child had two health cards: one with the history of the child's illnesses, vaccinations, and medical history in general, and one with the results of eye checkups, teeth checkups and vaccinations against influenza. I was extremely surprised the first time I filled out the history card (which had to be filled out every year of the child's attendance at the school) to find some very unusual diseases listed and that an astonishing amount of detailed information was required. Details were sought as to whether the child experienced any of the following:

- motion sickness
- dizziness
- waking up cranky
- palpitations when running
- catching colds easily
- frequent fever
- headaches
- tiring easily
- bad color
- eating a great deal between meals
- picking at food
- constipation
- diarrhea
- stomachache
- seizures
- frequent rashes
- eczema
- difficulty in hearing with discharge from ear
- difficulty in learning
- nosebleeds
- allergies
- blocked nose
- snoring
- frequent sore throats
- red eyes
- conjunctivitis
- squinting
- wearing glasses
- eyesight problem before entering school

Aside from the childhood diseases I had been used to dealing with, conditions like arthritis, kidney problems, and Kawasaki disease were also included. It was explained to me that many children in Japan developed arthritis around fourth grade because of the stressful life conditions associated with their extra study load. Kawasaki disease was new to me. This disease, otherwise known as febrile mucocutaneous lymph-node syndrome, mainly attacks infants under four years of age. Symptoms include high fever, bleeding of the lips, swelling of the neck lymph nodes, and inflammation of the palms and soles of the feet. The cause of the illness is apparently still unknown; it is named after Dr. Tomisaku Kawasaki, who first reported the syndrome in 1967. About five thousand cases are reported each year in Japan, of which between twenty-five and fifty are fatal.

Children were also vaccinated against the common Japanese cold. Notes were sent home from the school when several children in a class had colds, and parents were advised to have their children wash their hands and gargle frequently. When more than five or six children in one class were ill, the whole class was asked to stay at home for a few days and everyone was given homework to make up for the loss of study time.

Notes were often sent home to remind parents about the health care of their children. For example, when autumn came we were reminded to have our children wear undershirts, or that it was easy to catch colds. Similarly, at hay-fever time in the spring, notes were sent home advising the use of masks. They also reported the pollen count, obtained from the television news.

The Swimming Pool

Our primary school boasted a wonderful indoor swimming pool; all the children swam as part of the sports program, and used it more if they joined the school swimming club. Entrance to the pool was rigidly controlled: on swimming days a parent had to take the child's temperature before school, write it on the pool card provided, and sign with a *hanko* (personal seal).[8] At first, I used my normal signature instead of a *hanko*, but I found this a bit tedious and time-consuming. I was then given a personal hanko as a birthday present from one of the staff at my university and was most grateful for the convenience of it. I must admit to having put down Andy's temperature on occasions without having taken it. The card, duly stamped by the parent, was then countersigned by the teacher with his/her *hanko* before the child was allowed in the pool. Children had to undress in the dressing room and enter the pool in their school swimsuits through a foot bath first and then a shower. To avoid scratching other swimmers no watches or jewelry of any sort could be worn in the pool.

Modesty

Experience showed that the concept of modesty was entirely context dependent. As it is for most foreigners, the first experience in the public bath, or *sento*, had been interesting. Like most, I concluded that it is we foreigners who are apt to notice body differences of size and shape; the Japanese don't seem to focus on it at all. However, what I later found amusing was the absolute contrast of the Japanese attitude toward the body in the context of the public swimming pool. At the pool, the women would do contortions behind towels so as to hide their private parts, while at the *sento* they just stripped off and bathed naked. Japanese friends, when asked about this contradiction, at first laughed when realizing that in actual fact this does occur, and then explained that, when they thought about it, it was probably due to the association of the swimming pool with modern Japan, and of the public bath with traditional Japanese culture.

Bodily Functions

Much attention was given to the control of bodily functions. On the baseball team ski trip—a seven and a half hours ride—the bus stopped exactly every two hours, and all the children were asked to use the bathroom. At camp they checked the children's bowel motions, as described by Andy.

> One summer when I was at the YMCA summer camp, a very funny thing (or it seemed very funny to me) happened. It happened in the morning, just before breakfast. The leader of our group went down the row of beds asking some sort of a question. As the leader got nearer, I distinctly heard the word unchi (poo). I asked the boy who slept next to me, who could speak English, what it was all about. He said it was a poo check. He couldn't tell me any more because it was his turn. I had enough Japanese at the time to translate the conversation, and this is how it went between the camp leader and my friend.
>
> Leader—Hiroo, did any poo come out this morning?
> Friend—No, leader, no poo came out.
> Leader—(sssssssss) Well, go to the bathroom and try harder after breakfast. (tssssssss) I hope you're not sick.
> Next it was my turn and the same thing happened except that I said yes I had done poo, and the leader said "Good boy!"

Checking for Worms

Andy was very amused once when they checked the children for worms at school.

> One day at school an envelope with a note and a blue circle inside was handed out in the class. I had never seen

anything like it so I asked the person next to me what you do with it. When he said you stick it on your bum and bring it back to school I nearly fell off my chair. I went and asked the teacher and she told me the same thing. I didn't quite understand how to do it, so I went to the nurse and asked her. I understood her. So for the next two days when I got up, I right away went to the bathroom and stuck this blue circle of glue onto my bumhole. On the third day I took the blue glue in an envelope to school and put it in a big plastic bag with everyone else's envelopes in it.

Oral Hygiene

The schools were also very conscientious about oral hygiene, and keeping healthy teeth was a high priority.

Today we had an all-school meeting on teeth. A dentist came and talked to us about how and how long we are supposed to brush our teeth. After that the health committee gave a report on what the teeth do for you. It was basically:

> *Teeth chew your food*
> *Teeth help you speak*
> *Teeth make you look better*

We were also asked to bring a toothbrush to school, but for some reason all we did with it was to hold it up and see how many kids had brought their toothbrushes!!!

Hot Lunch

A wonderful feature of the Japanese primary school system was the lunch program, provided with meticulous research and detail into calorie count and nutritional balance of food. Parents paid about ¥4,000 [A$53, US$40] per month for this service, and the children received a hot lunch prepared in the school kitchen. An example of the menu for the month of December 1992 is given in figure 5.

PERFECTION AS THE ULTIMATE GOAL

In the primary school, children were encouraged to be as near to perfect as possible in all they did. Everything needed to look good, and this was achieved by encouraging great care and diligence.

Language

Perfection as the goal was especially evident in the study of the Japanese language, which was based on rote memorization and the correct way of producing a given message, especially in the written form. There was never any room for choice in language: what was produced was either good, or not acceptable because it did not conform to standards. The children were taught to form to perfection the characters in each of the three scripts in the written language. After the *hiragana* and *katakana* scripts (the two syllabic scripts) were learned, correct formation of the *kanji* (the Chinese characters) was reinforced through wonderful lessons in calligraphy, in which both the stroke order and the starting and finishing points of strokes were taught for perfect formation of the characters. It appeared, too, that a consequence of the emphasis on perfection was a focus on the form of a message or communication rather than on its meaning. It seemed to us that so much attention was paid to perfection of every detail that little attempt was made to deduce the meaning whenever the message was imperfectly worded. Frequently, a message in

Figure 5. Lunch Menu—December, 1992

DATE	CEREALS	DRINK	FOOD	CARBO.	PROT.
Tues 1	Cheese sandwich	Milk	Soup/5 ingredients Fruit	695 kc	29.8g
Wed 2	Margarine and bread	Milk	Prawn balls Chinese salad Fruit	699 kc	30.1g
Thurs 3	Soft french bread	Milk	Cauliflower cream Jelly	625 kc	22.5g
Fri 4	Rice	Milk	Roast meat Seaweed Potatoes in broth	699 kc	26.6g
Mon 7	Milk bread	Milk	Fried chinese dumplings Korean vegetables Sweet & sour ...	680 kc	22.6g
Tues 8	Potato sandwich	Milk	Pork soup Fruit	635 kc	22.4g
Wed 9	Fruit bread	Milk	Chicken with yoghurt sauce Boiled potatoes Vegetables	562 kc	27.6g
Thur 10	Shortening bread	Milk	Noodles Vegetable tempura Spinach mix	645 kc	21.8g

DATE	CEREALS	DRINK	FOOD	CARBO.	PROT
Fri 11	Rice	Milk	Tofu hamburger Japanese salad Fruit	698 kc	26.3g
Mon 14	Margarine roll	Milk	Curry stew Radish salad	672 kc	20.6g
Tues 15	Round bread	Milk	Fried fish with tartar sauce Baked potatoes Spinach & corn	661 kc	30.1g
Wed 16	Bread with jam	Milk	Macaroni gratin Green salad	702 kc	24.6g
Thur 17	Ham sandwich	Milk	Meat & veg. soup Fruit	575 kc	26.3g
Fri 18	Rice with 5 ingredients	Milk	Egg soup Fruit	601 kc	22.6g
Mon 21	Egg Roll	Milk	Spaghetti with meat sauce Vegetables Fruit	659 kc	23.7g

imperfect Japanese was simply ignored. Perhaps as a consequence of this emphasis on perfection in the native language, when English was required only those Japanese who were particularly confident would try to communicate.

Pencils, Not Pens

All work in the primary school was done in pencil, and indeed my students at the university also worked in pencil. This amazed me at first, until I realized that of course the point was to allow for presenting the perfect finished product. Hence, erasing was essential until one was satisfied.

Everyone Can Reach the Top

Perfectionism was achieved through promotion of appropriate values. Children were encouraged to strive toward the highest goals at all times. The underlying premise was not that each child was talented in different areas, but rather that anybody could succeed at anything provided he or she tried hard enough. In line with this thinking, children were taught to reflect frequently on where they could improve and to explain how they proposed to do this.

Teaching Styles

Orientation toward being perfect was the main difference we noted in the teaching styles of Japanese and Western teachers of the violin. The Japanese teachers would make the children learn a piece to perfection before they were allowed to move on to the next piece in the book. The Western Suzuki teachers would adopt a more moderate approach and allow the children to experiment by moving on faster, perhaps not producing equivalent standards of excellence.

Extra Time When Needed

It was also understood that the achievement of perfection often required more time than was allotted, either for presentation of content or for focus on the process of learning. Traditionally, ethics had been a separate subject in the curriculum of the Japanese primary school, but by the time we were involved, the introduction of ethics to the children had been melded into the process of teaching and classroom interaction in general. However, the subject "ethics" still appeared, interestingly, in one slot on the timetable, seemingly to provide extra time for whatever needed doing to achieve the standards of excellence required. Andy perceived the position of ethics as follows:

Q: Looking at this timetable, what's "ethics"?

A: Ethics is ... I think it's just a time that gets taken up ... with getting mad at somebody.

Q: What do you mean "getting mad at somebody"?

A: Well, if a teacher gets mad at a kid or something, the time that's wasted in that gets made up in ethics.

Q: So if the teacher gets mad at a kid during class time, then that's the time that compensates?

A: I think so, yes.

Q: So they don't actually teach you anything in that period?

A: Not since I've been there.

ATTENTION TO DETAIL

It appeared to us that in the Japanese primary school every activity was undertaken with attention to the finest detail. This was important at the individual level, as demonstrated in the calligraphy class description above, and was reflected in the organizational level.

Children's Safety

As already outlined, much attention was paid to the children's safety. To ensure that the first graders could be easily noticed by drivers, they were required to wear yellow hats instead of the usual white for summer and navy for winter, and had to carry school bags with a yellow cover on them. Children were not allowed to ride bicycles to and from baseball practice until they reached high school, and community members monitored the situation quite rigidly. Crossing guards were employed on a regular basis to control traffic at each of the main crossings near the school while children were coming and going.

Name Tags

Most items of the school uniform had a special printed stamp on them which allotted a place not only for the child's name, but the grade and school as well. Children were very much responsible for their own clothing, and uniform items were rarely lost.

School Property

Care and responsibility were also expected with regard to school property, such as the helmets hung by the side of the desks for use in time of disaster and the special uniforms worn by those serving lunch. Each helmet was the responsibility of the child sitting at that particular desk, and once each term it had to be cleaned. Those children on lunch duty had to wear a white smock and mop cap; at the end of their rostered week, these items were brought home to be washed and ironed for the following week's group.

Preparation for Camp

The detailed preparation that went into Andy's sixth-grade camp had to be experienced to be believed. It left me with no doubt as to where Japanese develop their careful and meticulous planning abilities. A meeting of the mothers with the principal and three accompanying teachers was held three weeks before the camp. At that meeting we were given details about all aspects of the camp, including our expected role in preparations. We were told that there were four main objectives for the children at the camp in Komoro, Nagano Prefecture:

> to spend time in, and to study, nature;
> to learn to act and live as a group;
> to take care of their own health and learn the rules of the camp;
> to communicate with the local people.

The camp was to last from early Monday morning until late Saturday afternoon; twenty-five boys and twenty-six girls would participate. The principal, three teachers, and two university students would accompany the group.

A list of items to be taken was given for each child: one large bag (for packing clothes and other necessities), one small bag (for hiking, to contain sketch book, etc.), clothes, socks, sweater, gym wear, pajamas, toiletries, a big towel and a small towel, rainwear, pencils, notebook (given by the school), thermometer (for taking daily temperature), sketchbook (given by the school), cotton gloves for manual work, packed lunch (for the bus), drink (for the bus), plastic ground sheet, treats for the bus (usually not many candies; mainly savory biscuits or rice crackers with seaweed), stamped, addressed postcards (to send to friends or family), apron and head scarf (for serving or cooking duty), watch and camera (owner's responsibility), school hat, name plate (for identification since two other primary schools would be at the same location), and name cards (to be made at school for various games introduced at the camp).

Some general preparations and advice were also outlined. The children were to start taking their temperature every day from the Monday the week before the camp, in an effort to begin a pattern of keeping track of their own health. All clothing was to be marked with both name and school. Children were to start a pattern of keeping to time schedules before the camp. On the day of the camp, if a child was not able to attend for any reason, the school was to be notified by 7:30. We were advised also that since Nagano is in the mountains, the temperature there is on average five degrees lower than Tokyo and could be rather cold at the end of October.

Then a list of deadlines was given. One week before the camp a copy of the family's health insurance policy, a green health card duly filled out, and the camp dues of ¥7,000 [A$92, US$70] plus ¥2,000 [A$26, US$20] spending money were to be brought to the school. A white health card would then be sent home so that each child could record temperature and bowel movements in some detail for a week prior to camp. Then at the end of that week, on the Friday before departure, the school doctor was to be called in, both to give a physical checkup and to check the information recorded on the white card. The green card, already filled out by the parents, contained virtually the same information that the school already had on file on the health card (required each year): name, address, telephone number, emergency telephone number, age, blood group, and whether the child regularly suffers from motion sickness, fever, colds, stomachache, diarrhea, asthma, dizziness, or rashes, takes special medicines, needs to be woken up during the night to go to the toilet, has ever had chicken pox, measles, German measles, mumps, appendicitis, or other diseases, and finally the guardian parent's expected timetable for that week so that contact could be made more readily in case of emergencies.

A detailed program for the camp activities was also given to parents, along with some final tips about making the children go to bed early for several nights before the camp and generally making sure they were physically fit. If the camp were to prove a negative experience, it certainly was not going to be through lack of preparation and attention to detail!

The Suzuki Method

The children's extracurricular activities were organized with similar attention to detail. Andy had been a Suzuki violin student in Sydney, before we moved to Tokyo, and was eager to continue in the Suzuki method. The Suzuki headquarters in Matsumoto had assigned us a Japanese teacher, but our Japanese language was so poor initially that this proved to be an unsuitable arrangement. We were lucky that there was an American teacher in Tokyo, and Andy became one of some thirty students she taught. The ideology underlying the Suzuki movement is representative of many of the values underlying Japanese education in primary school. The essential components of the Suzuki method are: an early start; a warm, supportive environment; listening; repetition and ability development; memorization by listening and repeating; parental input; lessons, group classes, and concerts; daily practice; parent and teacher training; small-step mastery (focus on the parts rather than the whole); one-point lessons (perfecting one point at a time); and tonalization.

Children can learn piano, violin, cello, viola, or flute in the Suzuki method. One parent is required to be responsible for the child's learning experience, and the parent must learn to play at least the most basic piece on the instrument with the child. After that the parent may choose whether or not to continue playing: most often the parental input after this point consists of sitting through the child's lesson with him/her and the teacher, taking notes, understanding the techniques and requirements for the child's practice, and being with the child during daily practice time. Children proceed quickly and with enthusiasm, following one weekly lesson and one group lesson each month. The method tends to produce students who are exceptionally well skilled mechanically but who, if allowed to pursue the method into mature years, play less musically and with a certain rigidity that other methods perhaps avoid. As an introduction to music it seems to be ideal.

The organization of both the Suzuki summer school and the national concert in Tokyo were typical of Japanese detailed organization. The first summer we were in Japan, in 1990, we attended the Suzuki summer school held in Matsumoto, northwest of Tokyo, where the Suzuki Talent Education Center headquarters are located. The summer school lasted four days, with a musical program each day from morning until night. Mothers and children are involved together, theoretically so that the mothers can provide the needed nurturing element. We began at 9:00 A.M. with small group (about thirty students) lessons on graded pieces until 10:30. From 11:00 until 12:30, all students met in the main hall and played in a large group. Each afternoon, concerts were given by students who had excelled, and, on one occasion, an evening concert was also held. On the other evenings, in the various *ryokan* (inns) where we stayed, Suzuki teachers organized group practices after dinner, in which all students willingly participated. My initial fear was that Andy would never endure such a rigid program, but the enthusiasm of all the students seemed to be infectious, and none of them wanted to return home at the end of the four days. There were very few non-Japanese students there—three, if I remember correctly—and there was great concern in the Suzuki organization as to whether we foreigners would be able to sleep on futons and eat Japanese meals! The Japanese are always concerned for the well-being of their guests and certain that foreigners will never be able to adapt comfortably to Japanese cultural practices.

Small group lesson at Suzuki summer school.

Afternoon concert.

Newly made friends at Matsumoto.

I had heard of the wonderful Suzuki National Concert which takes place in Tokyo each year in March, but was completely unprepared for the emotion I felt on our first participation, and indeed in each of the three years thereafter.

Approximately 3,000 children, some as young as two and a half, participate in this concert. Most play the violin but some play cello, flute, koto (a traditional Japanese lute), and piano. Approximately two months before the concert, Suzuki teachers begin having meetings to organize the event—understandable given the mammoth task involved. The students come from all over Japan, and a few come from overseas; they rehearse beforehand only once, in blocks of two hundred or so. Yet on the day of the concert, the most magical music is created. We were fortunate that the founder of the movement, Shinichi Suzuki, was still able to participate during the four years we were there; his inspiration to the children was inde-

The concert.

scribable. Even at age 95 (his age at the time of our last participation), he never refused a photo with any child, and addressed the children to inspire them in their music as he had always done.

Parent Participation

Parental involvement in the class and in PTA activities was highly structured and organized in every detail. Four main areas of concern had been nominated as important for parents' participation within the school. These were elections and communication, culture, the class newsletter, and children's safety.

Elections involved the rotational nomination of parents in the four positions. Communications was also part of this same portfolio, involving the telephone tree and notes home to parents. The telephone tree, a system in which one parent is delegated to call another until all have been reached, was especially important as a way to spread messages quickly in the event of emergency situations such as earthquakes, fires, or snowstorms. The person elected to the culture portfolio was responsible for organizing guest speakers, concerts, and excursions.

The class newsletter, issued once each term, published articles written by both children and parents regarding anything thought to be interesting—cooking and health were frequent topics. The safety mother's job entailed identifying any possible dangers in the area surrounding the school for the children in their comings and goings.

The head mother for the class was always the mother from the elections/communications portfolio. The four mothers representing the class, one in each of the four areas, worked with the representatives of the same interest group from every other class in the school. So, for example, the PTA safety group would consist of one representative from each class in the school. Several times each year the faculty would meet with the PTA representatives, and for that occasion each of the four interest groups would choose a representative. The PTA-faculty meetings were attended by the principal, the vice-principal, the head of the PTA, seven members of staff, two parents from the affiliated kindergarten, one parent from the handicapped children's class, and one parent representing the whole school in each of the four areas of concern.

Transition from Primary to Junior High

Great care and attention were paid to ensuring that the children felt comfortable in making the transition from primary school to junior high school. Some months before the end of the sixth grade year—in early December in our case—the children were all taken to the local junior high school, where the principal and some of the teachers addressed them. They were also introduced to the various procedures of the school, and were shown around. Many of the children were not sure at that time which school they would attend, and were in the middle of studying assiduously for entrance exams to private junior high schools. Nevertheless, the introduction to the public school was made so that all the children would feel comfortable about it.

ADHERENCE TO FORMULAIC PROCEDURE

Many Japanese practices seem almost ritualistic with their emphasis on appropriateness and form. The Japanese language is full of formulaic expressions, and mastery of them facilitates communication.

Meetings

As Andy explains, formulaic procedures were found in both the all-school morning meeting and the class morning meeting:

Q: This first meeting on a Monday morning, what's that?

A: Well, it's the whole school, and before the teachers come, the *shūban no sensei* talks. That's the teacher on duty for that week. She says, this week, for example, "Let's keep a handkerchief with us," or "Let's not be late to school," or whatever, and makes it a goal for the week. Sometimes they give us these sheets that you color in if you've done it right. And then the teachers come, and the *kōchō sensei* [principal] steps up and talks and steps down, and then we march out.

Q: And what does the *kōchō sensei* talk about?

A: Different things. Yesterday was a special day, so he talked about that day; or he might talk about what somebody said about the school and so let's *gambatte* [do our best].

Q: What kind of things do people say about the school?

A: Oh, they say it's a very good school and the kids always say "hello" and those kinds of things.

Q: And after the *kōchō sensei*'s speech you all march out, right?

A: Yes, to music.

Q: I see that everyday there is an *asanokai* [morning meeting]?

A: Yes, that's in the classroom. "*Kore kara asanokai o ha-jimemasu*" [Now we'll start the morning meeting].

Q: Who says that?

A: The *nitchoku* [two people who are designated class monitors for that day].

Q: And then?

A: *Kiritsu*. If the teacher is there.

Q: What's *kiritsu*?

A: Stand up. "*Ki o tsuke*" [Attention]. "*Ohayō gozaimasu*" [Good morning], and we all bow to the teacher and say *ohayō gozaimasu*. "*Chakuseki*" [Sit down]. "*Minasan kara no renraku wa arimasu ka*" [Does anybody have anything to say?]. "*Sensei kara no ohanashi desu*" [It's time for the teacher's talk], and then when the teacher finishes the talk, you sit down. If the teacher isn't there yet, we do the *renraku* part [Does anybody have anything to say?] first, and then, when she comes, do the "*ohayō gozaimasu*."

Q: And when she talks, what does she talk about?

A: Oh, you know, "Yesterday there was an episode" or "Please do your homework, whoever didn't do it."

Q: How does she know you didn't do your homework if you've only just come in then?

A: Because you're supposed to put it on the teacher's desk before. The doors open at 8:15, so we've got from 8:15 to 8:25 to put homework in and get all ready. Then you've got from 8:25 to go to the meeting, if there is one, and then you come back. The teacher always comes about five or ten minutes after the meeting, so you can put it in all that time, and of course when she says that, some people come up and say, "Oops, I forgot to put it in."

Q: So then the morning meeting is over after she's spoken?

A: Yes.

The same sort of ritualistic meeting was conducted each day before going home.

Q: There's a *kaerinokai* [closing meeting]?

A: Yes. "*Kore kara kaerinokai hajimemasu*" [We'll now start the closing meeting].

Q: And those same two people who did the morning meeting do the home-time meeting?

A: "*Minna kara no renraku ga arimasu ka*" [Does anyone have anything to say?]. "*Sensei kara no ohanashi desu*" [Now the teacher will speak]. Then she speaks. Then "*Kiritsu*" [Stand up], "*Ki o tsukete*" [Be careful], "*Sayonara*" [Good-bye], and that's the end.

Step-by-Step Guidelines for Procedures

The children seemed to expect a step-by-step procedure for whatever they did, and responded well to strong guidelines. The procedure for serving lunch is explained by Andy:

Q: Tell us about lunch.

A: Well, it's changed, but if it's in the classroom the *kyūshoku tōban* go down to the first floor. This is a group of four people that's in charge of the *kyūshoku* [the lunch].

Q: How often does that group change?

A: Once a week ... if it changed every day we couldn't have the serving uniform washed. They go down and get the lunch and bring it back up on a serving cart

in the elevator. Then they set it all up and ask everyone to come and collect it and take it back to our
seats. And when it's all done, the two day monitors
say *"Itadakimasu"* [the Japanese invitation to eat]. If
we're in the lunchroom, they set it all up and do it all
themselves and put it out on the table, then either
call everyone or, if we are already there, we just sit
down and, when we all are in the lunchroom, they
say *"Itadakimasu."*

Q: And when do they get dressed up in that white robe
and cap that you bring home every so often to wash?

A: Before they start. All four have to wear it.

Q: So what's the lunch like?

A: Good. Only a few things are yuck, like, for example,
in the salt bread they put too much salt or something.

Children learn to conduct the appropriate rituals themselves very early in the primary school system. As described earlier, the two monitors of the day (*nitchoku*) were
responsible for conducting the morning and closing meetings. The steps in the procedure for each were prescribed,
as was the exact language to be used.

Long Speeches

The children were used to listening to speeches of great
length, and often stood for long periods without complaining. Examples of two typically long speeches are the
opening address at the school assembly given by the principal, and the speech given before each baseball game to
the team by the head coach. Much of the time the children did not listen to what was said, and of course they

never questioned the function or usefulness of the procedure. They seemed to assume that the message, or the function of the ritual, lay in the behavior of conforming to a pattern, rather than in any informational substance.

Head coach of baseball team gives a speech.

No One Questions the Rules

Nor did anyone seem to question the many rules applied to everything. Often, when we could not understand the logic behind them and would ask, our respondents were not able to provide answers. The swimming pool is just one example. The school was fortunate to have a beautiful indoor swimming pool, which was also open to members of the community in the evenings and on weekends. In using the pool, the same rules applied for adults as for children. There were rules for using the locker room: one had to wear a cap and goggles; in entering the pool one had to pass through the footbath and shower; no jewelry was allowed; and one had to swim in the correct part of the pool in the appropriate manner. At the end of every hour, a signal would be given, and all swimmers were obliged to get out of the pool and sit for ten minutes while the lifeguards checked to make sure no one was on the bottom. Furthermore, no shampoo was to be used in the shower after swimming. When I asked why, nobody knew the answer, not even the pool lifeguards, who, every evening and three times on Saturday and Sunday, announced over the loudspeaker that under no condition was shampoo allowed in the shower. Eventually somebody in the ward office suggested to me that it was probably because of the drains.

In Japan, once you know the appropriate form or pattern—be it linguistic or behavioral—you are set. Thus in Andy's first encounter with the school, when he was asked to make a speech on stage in the assembly, he didn't yet know that he was supposed to say *"yoroshiku onegaishimasu"* and introduce himself.

Chapter 4

Socialization—
The Group

GROUP ORIENTATION

It became apparent almost immediately that it was most important to be part of the group. Unfortunately, what we did not realize was that, try as we might, we would never be considered part of that group. The socialization process was almost entirely organized around the group.

Class Committees

At the beginning of each academic year, children volunteered for the committees they wanted to serve on, both within the class and for the school. There was a committee for health, for looking after the animals, for the library, for art, and for all meetings, among others. Andy's impressions of these groups were as follows:

> The school's divided into groups. You've got the announcement group, the chicken poop-scooper group,

the sports group, the nursing group, the *kyūshoku* group [lunch group]....

Q: Is this the same as the class *kyūshoku* group?

A: No, this group is for the school, and they write up the menus on the blackboard and do the school *itadakimasu* [invitation to start eating].

Q: You belonged to the nursing group when you were in fifth grade, didn't you? Can you explain about that group?

A: We tell people at school meetings that they are doing something bad for their health, for example bad posture. We also do plays about health at meetings every now and again.

  The main part of the health group is the break duty. You are assigned one day of the week to stay inside and not play and to look after the room. By looking after, I mean that you have to sit and wait for people who are hurt to come to the nurse's room and help them.

Q: How do you know what to do?

A: The nurse teaches us.

Q: And when you are in one of these groups, how long are you in that group?

A: The whole year.

Q: There must be a lot of people in one group if it's the whole school divided up—320 kids in the school?

A: But it's only the fifth and sixth grades.

Q: So, on Wednesday afternoons you have a meeting for that, do you?

A: Yes, and when that's not on—it's only the second week in each month—we have a *daihyō iinkai*—and that's the representatives of each class, club, and *iinkai* [school committee] in one group; they make rules and stuff for the school.

In sixth grade, Andy chose to be part of the group responsible for making announcements over the internal communications network. This is how he describes it:

> *In the announcing group, we are supposed to divide up each day of announcing. The first step is that we divide the group into three: a group for Monday and Friday, one for Tuesday and Thursday, and one for Wednesday and Saturday. These groups each have four people. In my group we divide the day into four: one announcement in the morning, one at first recess, one at second recess, and one at the end of the day. As for the lunchtime announcing, we all go to it. At lunchtime, it depends on the day what we announce. The announcing committee decides what we announce, with a teacher present at the time just to make sure*

The announcing committee.

that we don't decide anything completely unsuitable. Al-
though the program changes every term, right now we have
the week's school program and the goal for the week on
Monday, request songs on Tuesday, more request songs on
Wednesday, a quiz on Thursday, and request songs on Fri-
day; since there is no lunch on a Saturday, there is no
lunchtime announcing. The request song announcement is
what most kids like. Kids from the school put their request
tapes in a request box. Then the announcing committee
group for that day takes out the tapes and plays them, also
saying who requested the songs.

School Clubs

The school also offered an elective club system which provided group activities for the children.

Q: Can you explain about the club period on Monday
   afternoon?
A: Well, there are sports clubs, a computer club ... lots
   of clubs.
Q: And do you have to belong?
A: No, it's by choice.
Q: And are the clubs popular?
A: Some of them are, some of them aren't. There's a dance
   club—that's popular with the girls but not with the boys.
Q: You've been in the swimming club—what did you do
   in that?
A: Swam [chuckle]. When I joined in fourth grade the
   pool wasn't ready yet, so we ran at Arisugawa Park to
   get strong, they said, and when the pool was done
   we'd do a few laps and then we'd work on something
   that day, like kicking.

Q: And this year in the basketball club what do you do?
A: We do *junbi taisō* [warm-up exercises] and then we have two matches among the four groups that we've made, and then we do *owari no taisō* [final exercises].

Groups in Sport

Groups were also the basis of organization on sports day. The running races were not organized as competition among individuals as they were in any Western school we have been associated with. Instead, the whole school was divided into two teams: the red team and the white team. Five pupils were selected to run in each heat, and the first, second, and third place finishers scored points for the team but no particular merit for themselves. The first-place winner did not then proceed to a final; there were no champions. The focus was not on the individual but on the group one belonged to.

In preparation for sports day many activities were carefully chosen and practiced. The fifth and sixth graders led a parade in which they all marched, each playing a musical instrument to form a band. Andy related the democratic way that pupils decided, with the teacher, which students would belong to which instrument groups:

> *I actually had a bit of trouble to get my trumpet part. I had tried out for three other instruments before the trumpet in the school band. I didn't like the other instruments so I dropped them. But there was another guy who wanted to play the trumpet who had only tried for two other instruments. There was a big debate in the class about who should do the trumpet. They said that the other guy should do it because he hadn't tried out as much. They decided to*

Red and white teams on sports day.

*take a test and make us both play the trumpet. Then there
was another debate about whether the test was fair. We
finally decided on a fair way. We took the test and I won.*

Marching on sports day.

Class Group Activities

Class group activities were also encouraged:

> *3 June 1993. Today I stayed after school to finish making some flowers out of* origami. *We [sixth grade] were making these flowers to hang up in the* genkan *[entrance] of the school. Each class has to decorate the* genkan *when it is their turn; the turns change every month. Because it is the rainy season, we decided on making a little boy walking in the rain with about six other different animals, all of them dressed up in raincoats. The flowers are to be put in the background and the foreground. We decided all of this (what to make, who makes it) between the whole sixth grade, with the* gakkyū-iin *[class leaders] organizing the discussion.*

The Class Play

A typical activity to foster group interaction and coordination was the preparation of the class play for the drama festival (*gakugeikai*), held every two years. The following conversation with Andy describes this activity:

Q: Andy, how was your class play organized?

A: Well, the teachers put out a script that they had chosen themselves because they thought it was good. It was about devils or something. Then they asked us to contribute any good ideas for a play to the class. One kid brought one called *Bokura wa umi e* (We Go to the Sea) and we chose that one. Then, because it wasn't the one that the teachers picked, because we decided ourselves, the teachers didn't have anything to do with it. There was no script, and we had to start from scratch using the story. So we had sixth-grade meetings and we did it by ourselves.

Q: How did these meetings go? Who controlled the meetings?

A: Well, first it was two girls organizing, but then a lot of the kids, especially the boys, were noisy so the teacher said that if somebody was naughty it might be a good idea to make them the leader.

Q: So the teachers were watching while this was going on?

A: Yes, of course. Otherwise we might not do anything. One of the naughtiest kids was noisy, so he became the leader, and of course we didn't get to do much. He flicked the blackboard duster at people's faces when they were noisy, so their faces became all white.

Q: So there was only one choice of script beside the teachers, right?

A: No, some other kids put things out, but we decided on that one.

Q: How was it decided?

A: "Who wants the kid's, who wants the teachers'," whichever had the most people. The others got considered, but there were three major ones ... I think there were probably about four, but one of them nobody voted for. I don't think many voted for the teachers' one, and it was between the two kids' ones. Then we started deciding who would make the script. About six or eight people put up their hands and volunteered. That afternoon was a holiday, and the day after, so they made it in that time.

Q: In a day and a half they wrote the play?

A: Um. They stayed up until three o'clock in the morning, I think. Some of them hadn't even read the book. Only one person had read it.

Q: Were these people who normally go to *juku* [cram school]?

A: Yes, actually. They brought the script to school and that day we just read through in turns taking whatever part came around when it came to us, a girl's part or a boy's part or whatever. It was really funny. One of the boy's voices has broken, and he got a girl's part—it sounded so funny!

Q: And then how were the parts given to people?

A: Whoever wanted to be what. We wrote it all out with a box beside it—the parts—and then wrote down the peoples' names who wanted to be that part. If there were two or more people, they read the parts and everyone voted. I tried out for the part of the math teacher against one of the girls and won. We took two periods to decide all this, and then we practiced the parts. By the next day we'd memorized it and we started doing it. We practiced one period a day, sometimes two. We had less than a month to do it all.

Q: And is the play going well?

A: Yes. There's a big thing on now. The words. They are like kids' words, and one of the teachers said he doesn't think that's going to be very good. We also decided the lighting, and everything.

Q: What's the story of your play?

A: Well, first of all some kids go to play in an open space where there's an old house, and they find wood and decide to build a boat with it. There are six big kids and three little ones. Two of the big kids aren't going to *juku*, so they take the two little brothers home, while the other four go to *juku*. (I'm the math teacher at *juku*.) The kids at *juku* say, "Hey, did you know that there's a typhoon coming tonight?" and then in the meantime the other two have taken the two little ones home. That night, when the typhoon comes, they go to save the boat and one of them gets hurt and his mother forces out of him where he was and makes him take her the next day, and the other kids are there. The other mothers go with her, and the mothers say, "You are not allowed to do this anymore." In the next scene, about a month later, all the kids, except the two that don't go to *juku*, are at school, and they say, "Oh, it was fun when we were making the boat, wasn't it, but I wonder where they went. The other two have gone somewhere and nobody knows where they are." And then in the last scene, the two are on the boat, saying, "Where are we?

Wonder how far we are off Japan."

Q: I know the other classes didn't write their own plays,
but explain the plays the other classes did.

A: The first grade did one about pirates; basically they
just dressed up and all ran on the stage and started
having a fight, did a dance, and ran off. Second grade
were tadpoles, and they were thinking what they'd become when they grew up. Third grade was about a
crow with black feathers; people were teasing him
about having black feathers, so he dyed them red first
because the monkeys said red was best because their
bottoms are red. Then some other bird came along in
the group and said it doesn't look very good because
it stands out too much, so he dyed them blue. Fourth
grade did "The Emperor's New Clothes." In the fifth
grade's there was a flood and these flying raccoons
wouldn't save the people. We didn't understand it
very well, and everyone said it was weird. The *waka-
take* [handicapped] children did a really nice play in
which they were birds and each wanted to be painted
a different color. They chose colors and were painted
by a painter, and all were content.

Support from the Group

Andy observed that when the children seemed to stick up
for you in a group situation, you first had to be either
very popular, clever, or funny, or else extremely out of it
in every sense. In his words: "You have to be either on the
top, or the bottom of the society. If you are in the middle
somewhere, it is very difficult."

Ideology also unites the group, as was shown toward
the end of 1993 when the debate about whether Japan

would open its market to foreign rice was going on. Each night on the television news, further developments on the issue were discussed in detail, and Andy would launch into an attack on foreign rice, saying that the taste was not nearly as good as Japanese rice and that foreign rice could be dangerous because of all the chemicals used in farming in other countries, that it would therefore be harmful to one's health, and that he would certainly not be eating any foreign rice. When I contested "his" views, his remark was, "Mum, you just aren't Japanese yet."

Camp

One of the four main objectives of the sixth-grade school camp, held in autumn of the final year of primary school, was "to learn to act and live as a group." All activities in the camp experience were encouraged with this objective in mind. The camp site was shared with another primary school, and many activities involved a local primary school as well.

The bus left for the camp site at 8:00 A.M. on Monday morning. The children had organized their own activities for the journey:

> When we got on the highway we started the games that we'd planned. The first one was a chain quiz, and the second was a guess the number thing. The third one, nobody would talk. It was ippun basu gaido in which someone has to become a bus guide for one minute. Of course the Japanese girls wouldn't do it and when it was their turn would say "Oh, no, hazukashii" [I'm shy] and so they wouldn't say anything. They kept on saying "Give me a minute to think"; then somebody at the back of the bus

*said that it was boring. Then we just talked to the person
next to us.*

Q: What time did you arrive there?

A: I think it was about 3:15.

Q: Was there a host school there?

A: No. It wasn't a school. It was a special place for
camps. We had the words for and from each other—
you know, a person from our school and a person
from the other school say something and end with
gambarimashō [let's all do our best]. Ours forgot to
bring his paper, his lines, so he just stood there. In
the end they asked him to go and get them from his
bag and everyone had to wait.

Then we went up to the beds and it was really
funny. They called it a bed but it was just a wooden
plank ... you know a normal bed has a wooden plank
with a mattress. This had a wooden plank with a cut

Camp sleeping quarters.

out rectangle in which was a tatami mat [straw mat] on which you pulled out a futon, and they called it a bed. We had a fire drill before dinner and after dinner we mucked around and played poker or blackjack or something. Then we had a talk about the *kōryūkai*, with the local school and another school. You know, a get-together. Then we went to bed.

The next day one of the teachers went around saying *"Hai, rokuji-han desu yo. Okite kudasai."* [It's 6:30. Get up, please]. Then we went outside to do the *asanokai* [morning meeting]. The principal talked and the teacher talked, and we did our exercises and then we rushed back in because it was freezing cold. On the second day the grass was frozen. It had ice on it. Then we had breakfast and cleaned the room. We didn't do it very well though because there wasn't enough cleaning equipment. I wiped the windows every time. Some kids didn't want to do it, so they went to the bathroom and said they were doing poo for thirty minutes.

So that first day we went out at 9:00 to a place which had a little zoo and some museums and a really beautiful flower show. Then we had lunch there and then went to the local school where we played basketball. Then we got these seeds. There was a bottom-base-stone and a top stone and it turns around and you put the seed inside. It gets all the skin off, and you can grind up the seed with the machine. While we were doing that the local school people used some powder that they'd made before and made a sort of a bread. While we were playing basketball they took a video and asked us our names and what we like to do. And then after we made the bread we all went to the lunch room and exchanged gifts. Then we ate the bread while watching the video they had made.

Each night, when we were ready for bed, we wrote what happened in the day and filled out the health card with our temperature and bowel motions.

The next morning we left the camp and climbed a mountain. It was really cold at the start but then of course got warmer as we were moving. It was quite hard actually. We climbed up for about three hours and down for about one. It was such a good view. There's a volcanic mountain called Asamayama, and it was right next to that. But if it had erupted it wouldn't have come to us because there was a valley in between. We had a perfect view.

Mountain climbing.

Then we went back and my group learned how to make music by blowing on a leaf. That night, after dinner, we explained this to the other group, and they told us how they had learned to make a straw horse at a farmer's house.

Learning to make music on leaves.

On the Thursday we did a sports meet. There were two parts to it—one hour in the morning and two in the afternoon—so we did the relays and then we made *gohan* [a meal] by making an open fire and making a sort of a soup called *tonjiru*. You put *miso* [soy bean paste] and pork and veggies and a lot of stuff in it. We ate it and, to tell the truth, it was a lot better than the cooking at the camp. Then we had to clean up for two hours. We then did the second part of the sports meet, which was soccer. After dinner that night, we went out in the freezing night and looked at stars.

On Friday we got ready for the *tanken-gakushū* [orienteering] for which we had had to make a course the night before. We had a map that two people from our group had made while we were cleaning up from making the soup on Thursday. So we followed this map and we were supposed to ask people when we got lost. We got an apple because we interviewed lots of places, and one that we interviewed was an apple-picking place. We were supposed to be back at 2:00, but everybody got back at about 2:45. Then we went apple picking and we were allowed to eat two and bring home the eight I gave you. Then we returned to camp and, after a bath and dinner, had a *happyōkai* [a meeting to explain what happened to the groups during the day].

An orienteering group.

On Saturday morning we got up and packed our bags, had a closing ceremony, and then left. On the way home we stopped at several places. I spent about thirty minutes at the lunch stop choosing a good *omiyage* [souvenir] for you, Mum.

ABILITY TO CONFORM

The Japanese are expected to conform to rigid rules for behavior and appearance. Just as there are acceptable ways of behaving in different situations, so there are also acceptable ways of dressing and styling hair. Accordingly, right from primary school, group conformity is continually enforced and individuality discouraged. We experienced several incidents which surprised and amused us in this regard.

Hankie, Tissues, and Fingernails

The primary school students were taught very early on to be prepared for all emergencies; one way this seemed to be done was to have them conform to behavioral patterns that would equip them in time of need. For example, one of the class committees had to do an occasional spot check on the other members in the class to make sure three requirements were fulfilled: each child should have fingernails clipped short, and should carry tissues for the nose and a handkerchief. The handkerchief served many purposes: wiping away perspiration, covering the nose and mouth in the event of fire, and drying hands in the washroom. The committee stood at the front of the class and called each student up to the front to be checked. Andy was not at all used to such personal control, nor did he remember initially how frequently these checks would take place, so the first few times he was caught out, especially where the handkerchief was concerned. One check day he noticed the monitor preparing, so he quickly told the person next to him that he had a runny nose and asked for a tissue. When the monitor called Andy's name for the check, it was discovered that he had borrowed the tissue from the person next to him, and he was told that one tissue wasn't enough anyway.

Clothing

The Japanese children seemed to feel comfortable in appearing and behaving like everybody else; they all seemed to want the same kinds of clothes, right down to their underwear. Andy was made very conspicuous by his underpants, which came not only in white, but also in bright red, blue, yellow, and green. The Japanese children all wore only white. On sports days or when they had medical checkups and had to change together, the Japanese children made fun of the fact that Andy had colored underpants. On these occasions he was nicknamed according to the color he had chosen; on days when he wore yellow, they called him *kaminari* (lightning) pants, and on days when he wore red, fire pants. This kind of teasing seemed to be much more concentrated in the Japanese school than in other schools he had attended, and it became a constant challenge to be sure to know which days were sports or medical checkup days, so he could wear one of his few pairs of white underpants. I say challenge because it was usually the mothers who organized what the children would take to school, following a bulletin addressed to parents which came home twice monthly. Of course, that bulletin was in Japanese, and although Andy could read slightly less than eight hundred kanji—the expected amount for fifth grade—this was not enough to read the bulletin. I received general translations by phone from a very pleasant mother who spoke some English, but I was reluctant to rely on her too much. The reader might well ask at this point why I didn't simply go out and buy several more pairs of white underpants. There were three reasons: there was the principle of the matter; the style worn by the other boys was strange to us (a square-shaped leg and an opening in front compared with the bikini style he had always worn); and I had bought a large stock of underwear for him when shopping back home and didn't wish to waste them.

There was no school uniform for daily wear in the Japanese primary school. However, there were certain uniform items which made students seem part of the group. There were two compulsory hats—a navy one for winter and a white one for summer—and notices were sent home advising the date on which children had to change from one to the other. First-grade pupils wore yellow hats all year round for safety.

There were uniforms for sports. The swimming uniform consisted of regulation swimwear, a cap, a wraparound towel, and a special bag in which to carry them. Andy found the swim trunks particularly distasteful as they were cut very high at the waist, and tight down over the hips and thighs, where he had been used to briefer trunks of a lighter, quick-drying fabric. For gymnastics and other sports, boys wore white T-shirts and white shorts. Girls wore the same T-shirts with very short navy briefs. Again there was a hat, which was red on one side and white on the other for team participation, and a special bag. The uniform, surprisingly, was bought at the local cigarette store, along with any school stationery requirements.

When Andy first joined the baseball team, he was given the number 23, and I duly sewed the two black numbers in the middle of the back of his white cotton uniform. The next year he was chosen to play first base and given the number 3; so, being a working Mum with not too much time, I heaved a sigh of relief and thought how wonderful it was that I need only remove the number 2 instead of sewing on new numbers. Alas, there is no rest for the *okaasan* (mother) in Japan: the first time Andy turned up to practice in that uniform he was told that it simply would not do and that his mother should remove the 3 and make sure she sewed it back right in the middle, instead of displaced slightly to the right as it had been. Single numbers had to be in the same position for everyone.

Equipment

Equipment also had to be the same for everyone. When Andy first joined the baseball team, having previously played on an American one for two seasons, he felt he needed a new bat. Having an inkling already of the Japanese way of doing things, I suggested he ask the *kantoku* (head coach), or at least one of the other coaches, which bat he should purchase. However, he asked the team captain instead, and the answer was that he could use any bat as long as it was wood and not metal. On the American team, appropriate bats were judged by the comfort of the weight, so Andy and I went down to the local sports store and tested various bats with the owner until one was duly decided upon and bought at considerable expense. Andy took it along to the following training session, but when he went to use it the coaches wouldn't allow it. It was heavier than the other children's bats, not surprisingly since Andy was a lot heavier than most of the other children on the team. Andy was devastated, and after much discussion among the coaches and children, it was finally the head coach who said Andy could use his bat for practice, but had to use a lighter bat for the game. I suspect this might have been because he would have been advantaged by the weight! All children had to have the same equipment.

The Lunch Box

Another area of conformity was the *obentō* (lunch) box. Although daily school lunches were provided by the school, an *obentō* was sometimes necessary for excursions, and it was often necessary to prepare a lunch for the Sunday baseball team matches. The preoccupation this caused Andy was amazing; I can identify readily with Karen Hill Anton, who wrote in *The Japan Times*:

> All kids seem to love it when their mothers make obento, and when my children need one, they're on my case to be up to snuff. *Umeboshi* (pickled plums) for button noses on a clown face of rice with bushy eyebrows of *nori* (seaweed), a mouthful of spaghetti in a little cupcake holder, and 12 other things all arranged just so in a box the size of a *tofu* (bean curd) container ... my youngest daughter Lila queries me the day before to make sure we have all the ingredients for a topflight *obento*. She checks off her list, and the last time she drew a diagram of how the food should be placed![9]

Like Karen, I too have had the diagram! Well-prepared

obentos are very important, and obviously Andy had been extremely embarrassed with the sandwiches and fruit I had regularly sent along.

There are few extended public holidays in Japan, but one of these is known as Golden Week, a period of several days at the beginning of May. During this period in 1992, when there were baseball games on successive days, I was asked to send fruit, in addition to Andy's *obento*, as my contribution to the coaches' lunch. I carefully peeled and quartered many oranges and spent considerable time setting them out decoratively in a nice tin before sending them along. Andy noticed that they were very much enjoyed by the coaches, but for some reason he felt the other mothers were not pleased. I dismissed his observation completely, but that evening I received a phone call to ask if for the following day I would change and send *onigiri* (rice balls, containing fish or pickles, wrapped in seaweed). Since I was working as usual and extremely busy, I sent Andy to the local sushi shop that evening to buy many *onigiri*. When he took them along the next day, they were apparently thrown in the garbage because they were not homemade!! The third day I was told not to send anything, and I was a little hurt.

Behavior

The broad training in academic and social skills that the children learned at school was also part of conformity. Much emphasis seemed to be placed on what was acceptable; even for a potentially creative activity such as making a video in social studies, the format was set down first. Similarly, when we participated in the baseball team ski trip, a rigid schedule was applied to the entire thirty-six hours, with little or no time for the children to play creatively in the snow.

Baseball team on ski trip.

Everyone, including parents, seemed to be expected to conform to the group behavioral norms, as demonstrated in an episode on a Sunday in October 1992. We went to the regular baseball game which mothers (and some fathers) attended. Up until that point I had been going to the matches with the other mothers in their cars. However, I found that I was wasting hours of time, both before the match started and afterwards, waiting for the children to be lectured by their coaches. I thus decided to ride my bicycle to the game, allowing me freedom in choice of when I wanted to come and go. This caused some astonishment on the part of the other mothers, not because a bicycle was an uncommon means of transport, but rather because I no longer went with the group.

Stature

At the school, two kinds of health cards were kept for the children. One was similar to those I have always had to fill out on entering Andy in a new school, although in the Japanese system it had to be filled out at the beginning of *every* year. It listed vaccinations, history of diseases, allergies, and the like. The second health card was an ongoing record of regular checkups at school. There were teeth checkups, eye checkups, screening for nits, and above all regular measurement of height and weight, which I found rather useful. Interestingly, though, the height and weight information was used to calculate a pupil's deviance from the norm using the formula of body weight over height cubed, multiplied by ten to the power of seven. The result of this calculation gave a figure which was put on a class scale according to five categories of too thin, thin, normal, fat, and too fat. The children seemed to take this very seriously: when Andy just made the fat category, he immediately put himself on a diet.

Conforming When There Are Two Groups

Whenever a new set of cultural values is embraced, one is often caught in the middle, not knowing quite which group one belongs to. With Japanese society expecting the children to conform and meld into the group, Andy felt, after some time at his school, a little uncomfortable in a situation where his Japanese friends met with a group of foreign friends. Our particular ward, Minato ward, was making boundless efforts toward "internationalization" and promoting activities in which locals interacted with foreigners. Indeed, the mayor held a meeting once each year with representatives from the foreign community, asking their opinions and suggestions. Schools were being encouraged to interact in exchange programs within the ward. The international school Andy had attended before moving into the Japanese primary school full-time had been using the Japanese school's swimming pool for its students' swimming lessons, and each school invited some students from the other to the annual fair or bazaar. In addition, the Japanese primary school accepted six of the foreign children as guests for three weeks at the end of June to help them improve their Japanese language skills. Andy found himself in the quite strange situation, in 1993, of being a guest in his old school, the international one, representing the Japanese one:

A: The international school gave us ¥2,000 [A$26, US$20] worth of coupons to spend, and when we got there all these kids started calling out "Andy," and I was a bit embarrassed in front of the Japanese kids. We went up to their sixth-grade classroom and there was a welcome speech by their teacher in English with one of the children interpreting. Then we divided into groups and it was a bit confusing because their school had numbered their groups 1, 2, 3, etc., and we had made ours A, B, C.... Then each of our groups of five was shown around by three of their students. They led us around the fair, but they didn't talk much, and then the girls in our group went off so we asked if we could too. So we went off by ourselves round the fair. I felt that my Japanese friends were a little bit childish compared with the international-school kids because the Japanese kids had their faces painted and went for the kindergarten activities.

Q: How did you feel going back to your old school?

A: Not very good. It's not so good to go back to an old place.

RESPECT FOR SENIORITY

The Senpai-Kōhai System

One of the fundamental principles of functioning in Japanese society is the belief in a hierarchical system of persons based on age, seniority, and position in the society. This principle is referred to as the *senpai-kōhai*, or senior-junior, system and operates throughout the society, from primary school to adulthood. In the company, employees know their position: they display appropriate behavior toward their *senpai* and command what respect they can from their *kōhai*. In school, the children begin to learn the system immediately, and it is inculcated throughout their primary school experience.

Fifth graders (*senpai*) getting to know younger students (*kōhai*).

Before entering the primary school, prospective first graders were given an orientation. For this event, the current fifth graders showed the prospective newcomers around the school for an afternoon. Each fifth grader was given the responsibility of one particular prospective first grader, thus creating a very special rapport between the two children. Then, when the new first graders entered the school the following year, there was a welcome ceremony during which the now sixth graders took care of their charges, automatically continuing the *senpai-kōhai* relationship.

The *senpai* position depended mostly on age, but you had to command respect to be actually given *senpai* status among your own peers. In Andy's fifth grade, a child who was particularly disliked would not command *senpai* status despite his age. The *senpai* status was acknowledged in linguistic devices and in behavior. For example, when referring to each other, boys used the suffix *-kun* when the teacher was present and no suffix when she was not; but if another boy was *senpai* the proper suffix was *-san.* They had to remember never to ignore their *senpai,* and had to speak respectfully. Andy, for example, got into trouble in fifth grade because he did not address a sixth grader using *san.*

Besides age, *senpai* status was determined by the status symbols of Japanese society. While in the international school, status symbols were the latest clothes and trips abroad, in the Japanese primary school they were cars and particular schools you had succeeded, or might succeed, in entering. Sometimes contact with foreigners was also perceived as a status symbol, but this depended on the group of people concerned.

Strength was another factor that determined status, and was demonstrated in the early stages of Andy's arrival at the school. Soon after he started on a part-time basis, the strongest boy in the class challenged him to a fight over an unimportant issue, seemingly as an excuse to prove his strength. One of Andy's advantages in this kind of situation was his size and his ability to use it to his advantage. On this occasion, although Andy came home with skin off his face, he had won the fight by pinning the other boy's hands behind his back and laying him flat across the table. The interesting thing about this episode was that one of the teachers had been in the adjacent classroom and waited for the outcome without intervening in any way, as a Westerner perhaps would have, to stop the children from hurting each other. At the end of the fight the teacher asked each child to apologize to the other to conclude the episode. The Japanese boy refused, but the next day came to school and apologized immediately.

The *senpai-kōhai* system was used throughout the primary school system in many ways. Here, two examples from the baseball team illustrate. One Wednesday afternoon Andy had to stay late at school for the nursing committee and was thus late for team practice. Knowing that the Japanese are always very punctual, I asked Andy whether the coaches were angry when he arrived late. He explained that it was never discussed with them directly. What happened was that, when a team member arrived late, he gave his excuses to the other team members and particularly to the team captain. If the others judged that the excuses given were not acceptable—for example, a particular member had been playing or watching television— they would talk in loud voices so that the coaches could hear and the member would be punished. If, on the other hand, the excuse was deemed valid, as in Andy's case, then the discussion would go no further than the other team members.

Leadership

To be baseball team captain was, of course, a great honor. Part of the responsibility of being captain was to take the glory when there was a win, but also to lose face if mistakes were made. When Andy first joined the team, I was very surprised to see this in action. After a game one day I was standing with the other mothers behind the team, listening to the coaches reprimand the children for their bad performance in having lost a game. One of the coaches, singling out specific team members for specific deficiencies, hit the team captain over the head so that he stood there crying in humiliation and, I imagine, pain (although Andy says they don't feel pain). I was actually standing next to the captain's mother and expressed my concern—she just laughed and said that that was the procedure when the team lost.

Children were rotated in positions of authority to have them practice interaction in different positions of leadership. Andy describes class-leader positions within his grade:

> *A* gakkyūiin *is a leader in a grade. In our school there are two classes [called* kumi*] for each grade. There is one boy and one girl* gakkyūiin *for each class. They change every term. The responsibilities of the* gakkyūiin *are to answer the phone when the teacher is not in the classroom, to chair discussions, and to make decisions when the teacher is not there. For example, this morning the teacher was copying a*

worksheet and was late. In the time that she was gone, the gakkyūiin *made a decision that everybody should be doing* kanji *practice. If the students don't accept the* gakkyūiin'*s decision, it is the* gakkyūiin'*s duty to tell the teacher. It is also the* gakkyūiin'*s duty to tell the teacher when people are noisy when the teacher isn't there. Our class's boy* gakkyūiin *has not been decided on, so I am thinking of becoming it. But, they might not want me to be it.*

Teachers and Parents

The primary school seemed to assign a nurturing role to the teacher above and beyond what we had been accustomed to in the schools with which we had previously been associated. In Japan, any teacher holds a status far superior to that of a teacher in the West. Indeed, the term *sensei* in Japanese—the Chinese characters mean "born before"—is assigned to doctors, lawyers, and any other members of the community deemed to possess wisdom or power.

Teachers seemed to dedicate their whole lives to the welfare of the children they were teaching. In Andy's school, each teacher usually stayed with the same class for two consecutive years, which of course allowed time to get to know each child extremely well. The school was always open until late at night, with children able to go back at any time to retrieve essentials left behind, such as homework instructions. On one occasion Andy returned to school after dinner, at about 8:30 in the evening, to collect some math pages, and met both the principal and the vice-principal still working. The principal asked Andy why he had returned and advised him to run along home since it was getting late.

The class teacher seemed to nurture the children as a

mother would, and the children developed a very special relationship with her. In my first experiences of this I reacted almost jealously, until I came to appreciate the care being given. Even so, there were a number of occasions when I resented the intervention of the teacher in communication between myself and Andy. I had always brought Andy up to be as open as possible in his communication with me, with his first loyalties to the home. He became a little confused when the teacher asked him not to tell his mother about some events in the classroom, especially since these were always associated with disciplinary measures at school. While the events themselves appeared so unimportant to me that I cannot even recall the details, the fact that he was directed to side against his mother was somewhat confusing for Andy, and a source of conflict for me.

In the parent-teacher relationship, status and role were well defined. There seemed to be few opportunities for public expression of opinion or concern by parents, either through students or directly, as was demonstrated in an incident that occurred during preparation for Sports Day when Andy was in sixth grade. It had been decided that the sixth grade would do human pyramids for Sports Day, and they had been practicing every day for some time. I had very recently read several reports in which children doing human pyramids in the United States were described as having sustained severe injuries when the pyramid collapsed (the finale to the exercise). I quizzed Andy on the procedure and explained to him that, as long as they jumped each member off one by one at the end, there was little danger, but that I did not want him on any account to participate if the finale was a collapse, particularly since he, being one of the biggest boys in the class, was always positioned on the bottom. I told him that if they were instructed to collapse, he was to excuse himself politely to the teacher and explain that his mother did not want him to participate. Three days before the Sports Day, the teachers decided to collapse them. Andy excused himself, causing chaos. The teacher had been made to lose face and was extremely angry. She tried to insist that Andy participate, but Andy insisted he could only do so if they were jumped off as before. We were not quite sure how to handle this situation of conflicting values. That night I telephoned my particular confidante among the Japanese mothers, and she advised me that it was better for Andy and me to withdraw from the Sports Day on the pretext of being sick than have the teacher lose face in this way. A foreign acquaintance, a teacher herself, married to a Japanese man and with three children, who had all been in both Japanese and international schools, advised us not to have Andy present for the event, suggesting that we leave just before it on some pretext, rather than create embarrassment to the teacher. For some reason, the teacher finally decided to have the children jump off after all, and Andy happily participated. Afterwards, several mothers came up to me at the sports day and said they had shared my feelings about the issue, but had considered it inappropriate to express their concern.

SENSE OF DUTY AND OBLIGATION

As a result of the *senpai-kōhai* system, children quickly learn a sense of duty and obligation at an early age. Duty and obligation were paid and received appropriately between individuals within a group; by committing yourself to the group, you seemed to have to accept that you were bonded in very special ways. Each child learned very quickly where their obligations lay and what sort of behavior was expected in consequence. As a mother I found it very difficult to assess exactly what was expected of us in this regard, and felt very inadequate in guiding Andy.

One example was the way the sixth-grade graduation was organized. In Japan, graduations from kindergarten, from sixth grade, junior high school, high school, and university are all extremely important. Having been part of the school group for a considerable period of time, you are therefore bonded to it. Indeed, Japanese are known to attend reunions with primary school friends even in their retirement years. At the time of graduation from each of these levels, it is customary for the group to show gratitude by presenting the school with a gift, which remains as a token of their attendance. These gifts are usually very carefully thought out, with practicality the primary criterion, as in the case of the 1992 graduating sixth grade, which gave cloths to cover the lunch trolleys in the dining room. In addition, a big graduating party was held and a beautiful photo album prepared for each sixth grader as a souvenir. Parents, of course, had to pay for all this, and we were asked for ¥27,000 (A$355, US$270) in Andy's graduating year. Andy was beginning school in Australia, and because the Australian school begins in February and the Japanese school finishes at the end of March, Andy was not able to attend his graduation ceremony and party. The Japanese were appalled at such a thought, and asked me to consider flying him back for the occasion, since it was an event of such significance to them.

It was very difficult to understand some of the spirit of gift-giving in the light of these feelings of duty and obligation. In June 1993, I was at a loss to know what to do for Andy's birthday. I first suggested to the teacher, through Andy, that we have some games and a mintie (a popular Australian candy) hunt and a cake after school in the school grounds for the class, but the feedback was that Japanese children do not celebrate birthdays in that way. Indeed, birthdays were only recognized by the school in a group announcement at the beginning of each month. Since Andy and his friends were very keen on baseball, I decided to take him and six friends to a game at the Tokyo Dome with some tickets I had been given. When we arrived we found that the tickets were intended for unreserved seats especially set aside for cheering, and that these had been filled three hours before the game, so we were left standing. Visualizing the difficulties with seven children and myself standing for three hours for the game, I paid ¥2,300 (A$30, US$23) per person for seats. The children had a wonderful time. As I found out later, Japanese mothers rarely take more than two guests of their children at one time anywhere. I was left with no doubts as to the reason when I witnessed the exuberant behavior of the Japanese children as they swung from rails in the train and teased other passengers on the way home. I pretended I was not with them most of the journey and was rather relieved to return home without major mishap. The mothers evidently felt very much in debt to me over such an invitation, and wrote notes and sent flowers and fruit as thank-you gifts. Whether this was just a normal thank-you or whether they thought I had made myself a martyr, I'm really not quite sure.

Returning on train from baseball game.

Gift-giving in Japan has its own special ritual, and I'm afraid I was always on the learning curve. Souvenir gifts were always expected on return from holidays, which proved rather expensive and time-consuming when you thought of everyone with whom you interacted on a daily basis. On the other hand, it was not considered appropriate to give personal gifts to teachers, as we had done in international schools at the end of the school year and at Christmas.

Obligation and duty created strong, sometimes lifelong bonds between teachers and students, and as teachers became old and infirm, former students would often visit them and show care. A sense of obligation and duty similar to that of a family pervaded the life surrounding the school, and inculcated in the students the basic values underlying the networking process so essential to operating in Japanese society.

Obligation to the group also took precedence over any individual considerations at all times, as was demonstrated to us on numerous occasions. Andy was asthmatic, though at the time was no longer experiencing the frequent attacks he had suffered as a two- and three-year-old. But particularly when the seasons changed in Tokyo, he, like many of the Japanese children, was susceptible to quite strong attacks. One of these occurred during an unusually cold spell in September 1993, and indeed many Japanese children were hospitalized at the time. Andy had had to stay away from school on a Wednesday; Thursday, the following day, was a public holiday. Most holidays were taken up with the baseball team, and a game had been scheduled for that Thursday. However, when I woke up it was raining and cold; I decided that it wasn't appropriate to send Andy to play and that, since the game would certainly be cancelled anyway, there was no need to advise anybody. Half an hour after he was due at the field, however, I received a phone call from the team captain's mother asking why he wasn't there; when I explained that he had been away from school sick, and that I didn't want him out in the rain and cold, she was appalled. She said that the team would lose if he didn't come because they didn't have enough players, and insisted that he present himself. He very reluctantly dressed and went by taxi. When he arrived, he found that there had been enough players, but that they were afraid of being beaten by the scheduled opposing team, which was reportedly very good. They won the game, but no one thanked Andy for making a special effort to go. It was seemingly just part of one's duty as a team member, a member of the group.

AWARENESS OF GENDER ROLES

Despite much attention in the home studies program to teaching both boys and girls the domestic arts, we felt that gender roles were promoted mainly through role models presented to the children in the community.

In Japanese society, the male and female roles still seemed distinctly defined. Mothers were largely expected to stay in the home and be responsible for the children's education, and the majority of them were happy to do so. The society in general, and the education system in particular, relied on their support. With the high level of literacy in the society, most mothers seemed to forgo what in the West might have been personal fulfilment in a career, and to inject their high level of learning into preparing their children to take their places in the society in the next generation. However, the children generally did not seem to have much respect for their mothers. On one occasion the teacher asked the children to choose an animal to represent their mothers and give reasons for their choices. Most children in the class chose the pig and said their mothers were fat and bossy. At least Andy chose the leopard, saying I had similar spots on my face and always rushed around very quickly doing things!

Parents seemed to have very little direct input into the academic preparation of their children at the school, and most interest was taken by the mothers. Mothers attended parent-teacher interviews and went to the school several times each year when parents were invited to watch the teacher giving lessons. On each occasion that I attended these observations, the others participating were mothers. Most of the activities in which parents could take part were scheduled in the evening, when most of the fathers were unavailable. Even on the one occasion that a meeting was scheduled on Fathers' Day, fathers did not participate. For weekend playground activities, however, fathers were often organizers, as they were also for team activities and annual events such as concerts and the school bazaar. In fact, bazaars, concerts, and sports days were usually held on Sundays to allow the fathers to be present, and the following Monday was declared a school holiday. This, of course, favored the participation of working fathers, but did nothing for the few working mothers, who then had to make child-care arrangements for the children on the Monday.

The deference of the women to the men was demonstrated on many occasions, one of which is described in my diary entry for Sunday, 11 October 1992:

> The most astonishing thing today was the lunch at the base-ball ground. We were all asked as mothers to bring something for the obentō [lunch box], and I didn't really know quite what I was supposed to be preparing. Anyway we got there and, as on every other occasion, the mothers had prepared the most exquisite luncheon, even to the extent of bringing the teapot and then the hot water in a special container and little cloths and the chopsticks and everything. By 12:30 the mothers were all starving and the game was still going on. They laid out the food on the bench in the park, and I asked them why they didn't start eating. They replied that they couldn't eat until they had given the food to the coaches first. So they waited until the coaches came off the field, they served them until they had finished eating, and then when the men had had a cup of coffee to finish

and moved away from the spread, the mothers ate what was left.

Attitudes of men to women were evident at the swimming pool. The school pool was open during non-school hours at specific times to members of the community for exercise. During those times, the pool was divided into three sections. The first, which had an access ramp, was set aside for the handicapped and very small children learning to swim. The middle section, which was the largest, was for those walking or swimming slowly. The last section, one lane only, was for those serious swimmers wanting to do laps and was designated the training lane. When I went to the pool each Sunday afternoon, so I joined the training lane to do my forty laps for exercise. On Sundays this was also frequented by a lot of men, presumably getting fit before the week's work, as I was trying to do. Like all things Japanese, there were rules for this section, very similar to those for driving a car. You had to go up the right side each time, and only pass a slower swimmer when there was no "on-coming traffic." There was an orange line about four meters from the start to indicate the appropriate distance between one swimmer and the next. The women were very respectful of these rules and, if they were slower or faster than you, were very cordial about changing places. The men, however, swam on regardless, bumped into the women, never apologized, and rarely observed the rules. Needless to say, the five lifeguards on duty at any one time said nothing to the men, but often reprimanded women for the most inoffensive behavior, such as accidentally infringing on another's space.

In the Japanese primary school, children seemed in general to develop interest in the opposite sex later than in the international school. Already in third grade at the international school, the children were being encouraged by teachers and parents to give Valentine's Day presents, write notes to each other, and generally focus on who might be interested in whom. By the time Andy left, at the end of fifth grade, many of the children were paired up and had started dating to movies and dances. In the Japanese system, there were only rare, isolated cases of any such interest being shown, and this was not encouraged by parents or teachers. In discussions between some Malaysian students and Japanese students at our university, both groups said that they did not have any interest in dating until at least junior high.

It seemed to me that, where the Japanese girls were concerned, little consideration was given to the shyness that accompanies development in puberty. The girls' kindergarten sports uniform consisted of loose boxer shorts and a T-shirt, while that of the girls in the rest of the school, including fifth and sixth grade, was a similar T-shirt and some extremely tight pants similar to underwear that, for adolescent girls, seemed to be unnecessarily revealing.

COMMITMENT TO THE GROUP

In the Japanese primary system, children were taught very early that any commitment to a group activity such as baseball, or a personal goal such as passing an exam, was an all-or-nothing commitment. The spirit of giving your whole self to the cause prevailed. This was shown to us on several different occasions.

The first was the baseball team. Most Japanese children

seemed to make only one extracurricular commitment, so mothers seemed to find it unusual that Andy did both Suzuki violin and baseball. The two activities were always in conflict, as the baseball team members would be called on without prior notice and there would often already be a commitment to perform in a violin concert. It was always very embarrassing trying to make the excuses on these occasions, and Andy was made to feel that he had let the team down on the occasions when he chose the violin.

The Suzuki movement took a similar approach to commitment. Most of the Japanese children who elected to do the violin were doing at least twice as much practice per day as Andy and seldom took on an extracurricular sports activity as well. I remember meeting the mother of a boy the same age as Andy at a function in the first year we were in Japan. When she discovered that Andy studied Suzuki method violin, she told me that her son was at the stage of Book 8 (the Suzuki levels are measured in books, and Andy was on Book 3). She said he was practicing two hours each day (compared with Andy's thirty minutes) and that he travelled to Tokyo from Yokohama each week for his lesson, which began at 9:00 P.M., and rarely arrived home before 11:30 P.M. on lesson days. The rewards for this kind of dedication were to be found in the commitment of the Suzuki teachers, and of course of Suzuki *sensei* himself, the founder of the movement. As each child in Japan graduated from a level, a performance tape was made and sent to Dr. Suzuki in Matsumoto. Up until the end of 1991, when he was 93, he listened to each one himself, passed or failed them, and recorded lengthy comments on the tape explaining deficiencies and making recommendations to the child. I am told that he used to get up at 5:00

Andy with Dr. Suzuki.

each morning to begin these assessments, before his daily schedule began.

The children who were intent upon passing the entrance exam for a specific, private junior high school were entirely committed to their study for that exam. While Andy was at school in Japan, we commuted to Singapore for school holidays; when Andy was in sixth grade, he had wanted one of his friends to join us for a short period during the six-week summer vacation. We did not realize when we issued the invitation that his friends planned to spend the summer of sixth grade chained to their books from morning to night!

As with most experiences in Japan, that of being an active member of the PTA was usually intense. I was interested to read in *The Japan Times* (20 June 1993) about the experiences of a Japanese mother who had worked in the PTA both in Japan and in the United States. In comparing the two experiences she remarked that she had been "stunned by the contrast." She felt that whereas her experience in New York had been of a relaxed atmosphere in which mothers volunteered their services and things were very casually organized, in Japan there was so much emphasis on formality and doing things the correct way that people were very "uptight" about their participation. She described a meeting to arrange a sixth-grade farewell party for teachers, where PTA members haggled over who would be the master of ceremonies for the occasion, with no one willing to volunteer because the slightest mistake would be frowned upon. After that, the meticulous organization of the event required members to be assigned duties such as attending to the teachers in the waiting room, leading the teachers into the banquet hall, and organizing the seating order. The Japanese woman didn't say that the American style was necessarily better, but pointed out that everyone was so afraid of committing errors in organizing the event in Japan that it all became extremely tense. Group organization always required total dedication and commitment.

COMMUNITY SPIRIT

Community spirit was nurtured both inside the school itself and in the wider community of which the school seemed to form the nucleus.

Lifestyle

On moving out of the embassy and its protective environment, our whole life changed. As we gradually learned how to function in Japanese society, we came to have less and less to do with our expatriate friends, whose lifestyle simply did not synchronize with our all-consuming Japanese lifestyle. American friends would phone us a week or ten days prior to the occasion to invite us to Sunday lunch. We would never be in a position to accept, since we never knew what the baseball program was until a few days before—sometimes even just one day before. It was almost always impossible to go away for a weekend, as invariably Andy had school on Saturday and other school-related activities over the weekend. As part of the community, our whole life seemed consumed by it.

The first thing we had to adjust to in our move was the size of our apartment—bedroom, living room, bathroom, and kitchen—thirty-four square meters in all. The comparison is always relative: while we were comparing with a former expatriate lifestyle, by Japanese standards our home was reasonably spacious for two people. Along with the new size came all sorts of practical adjustments. In the embassy we had had a small laundry room with a washing machine and dryer, but out in the real world, flats were so small that the washing machine was often placed outside on the balcony, and dryers were more the exception than the rule. Our apartment block had a laundry room on the third floor, with one coin-operated washing machine to serve fifteen apartments. There was in fact a dryer too, but it generally took from three to six hours to dry towels, for example, so that the cost of laundering our weekly bath towels ran to ¥1,000 [about A$13, US$10] at the time. I was certainly glad I only had one child, as life was a constant juggle of hanging laundry on racks and hangers all over the two rooms to catch sunlight so as to dry things as quickly as possible. My main bone of contention was always the baseball uniform, made of white cotton, which inevitably came home black from sliding in the mud and had to be first soaked, then scrubbed, then washed, dried, and ironed. I began to understand why being a Japanese mum was a full-time job!

Initially, my main worry was how Andy would fare in such a change, and particularly where he would spend his spare time. I visualized us going mad living in such close quarters, but I had little idea of the school's function in relation to the home. Just as the office functions as home for its employees in Japan, so the school functions as home to its pupils, and much of Andy's spare time was spent at the school with his friends.

Safety

In the public school system in Japan, because you are legally required to attend the primary school nearest your home unless special negotiations are made, the school becomes the center of the community. Dangers for the children are minimized because everyone in the area with children knows each other, mainly through the school. If a child were to get into danger, or create it, the situation would immediately become common knowledge in the community. Committees of parents from our school's safety group monitored the area for dangers and reported any possible new ones to the school. Notes were often sent home warning parents of corners recently recognized as dangerous, or streets which had become very busy. At the beginning of each school holiday, parents were reminded about the dangerous areas for children riding bicycles and playing.

The Japanese were particularly conscious of the safety of the children while in the school environment, a situation exacerbated by Japan's vulnerability to natural disasters, particularly earthquakes. Schools in Tokyo were especially well organized in this regard. Once each month there was a drill focusing on escape procedures in case of earthquake, fire, flood, typhoon, snow, or any other disaster:

> *The school siren goes for a bit and then the Vice Principal announces on the school announcing system where the fire is if it is a fire drill, and if it is an earthquake drill he says how strong it is and where to go. As we walk down the stairs we are supposed to do three things: "Be quiet," "Don't panic," and "Don't push." All the students are timed by the Vice Principal to make sure we escape as quickly as possible. We usually "escape" to the playground, but we sometimes "escape" to Arisugawa Park.*

The class telephone tree was particularly designed to facilitate communication in these types of emergency situations, and mothers (or other family members) were supposed to be on hand to pick the children up at the designated place after the drill.

Special consideration was also given to the safety of the children outside school hours. A typical paper sent to parents at the beginning of the summer of 1992, about how children should take care during the summer, gave tips as follows:

Rules for a good summer life

1. Let's observe pool hours.
2. Let's keep to the designated route going and coming from the pool.
3. Let's go straight home after swimming.
4. What we can do by ourselves, let's do by ourselves.
5. Let's not arrange to play with friends before 10:00 in the morning.

6. When told we've done something wrong, let's not do it anymore.

Let's have a bright and healthy summer

Participate in the pool activities.
Make our body healthy (radio exercises, jogging).
Avoid photochemical smog (listen to the radio announcements and stay indoors when smog is particularly bad).

Let's make a study plan

Choose a reasonable study plan.
Read a lot of books.

Let's have a fun and safe time

When coming to school, don't come by bike.
When lighting fireworks, have an adult present.
When asked by a stranger to get into a car or follow, don't go.
Don't go to dangerous places or those places where children are not allowed (game centers, construction sites, shops open at night).
Respect the rules of the road, try not to get into accidents (respect the traffic lights, don't play on the roads).
Be careful and safe when riding bikes (get a parent's permission before going far away).

Care of the School

A caring attitude towards the school was developed in the children by teaching them to participate in maintaining it. Thus, the regular cleaning in the school was done by the pupils: Andy had to dust, vacuum, and anything else required. These responsibilities were quickly reflected in behavior in the home, as witnessed by an exchange between Andy and myself after he had been full-time at the primary school for six months. I hadn't been able to clean the house on Saturday, as was my usual practice, because of a seminar. I remarked to Andy that the house was dirty, and he quickly replied, "Yes, I suggest the system is wrong. We should do a fifteen-minute *sōji* [cleaning] each day."

Cleaning at school is described by Andy as follows:

Q: Will you explain how the cleaning's done?

A: Well, the class is divided into four groups of six, and [we clean] in rotation: classroom, central staircase, left staircase, and the gymnasium.

Q: So explain what happens if you have to clean the gymnasium?

A: We have to mop the floors and the stage, and it's only our group that does it, but sometimes you get the dust off the basketball hoops and go up on the second floor part.

Q: So each class has responsibility for different areas in the school, right?

A: Yes. The whole school basically.

Q: What about the *genkan* [entrance]?

A: Well, the *genkan* [cleaning] was stopped last year because naturally kids want to play, and when they do play, people outside see, and [the teachers] say it's bad for the school's reputation.

Q: When the kids play when they are supposed to be doing this *sōji* [cleaning], what do they do?

A: Well, sometimes they hit a ball around with a broom

and play hockey ... bump into each other with their mops and go *"Don, jan ken poi,"*[10] and if you lose you have to move out of the way, and stuff like that.

Q: So you think the kids don't like doing the *sōji* much?
A: No ... nobody likes cleaning.
Q: Do you have to clean the toilets as well?
A: No. The cleaning lady does it.

An extension of the school as home was its involvement in the community.The primary school had an obligation to have the children clean up the local park once a month. When Andy first had to clean the park, he was most disgusted because all the Japanese children had brought gloves from home, and he hadn't been prepared but was obliged to pick up the rubbish anyway.

Pets at School

Most primary schools seemed to keep pets. I have seen ducks, guinea pigs, rabbits, chickens, hamsters, birds, and tortoises at primary schools during my time in Japan. At Andy's primary school there were rabbits, chickens, and fish.

There was an *iinkai* (school committee) responsible for feeding the rabbits and chickens and cleaning their cages. With this care for the pets came the joys of seeing the newborns and watching them grow, with the subsequent concern for their welfare, as the following incident described by Andy shows:

> At school, there is a rabbit cage with a fenced-in play garden attached together with a door. One day a rabbit had babies. In the afternoon when everyone had gone home, the janitor lady saw the mother rabbit in the play garden and

shooed the mother rabbit inside the cage. But, she hadn't seen the mother rabbit's babies still outside. The next morning, the group in charge of animals went to the cage and saw the mother rabbit without her babies. Then they saw the two babies in the play garden. When the group in charge of animals put the babies back in the cage with their mother, the mother didn't recognize them. Because the rabbit mother and the rabbit babies had spent their first night separated, the mother didn't know the babies anymore. Our class teacher at the time was the lead teacher of the group looking after animals, so she brought the babies and the mother to the classroom in separate boxes. Every hour she held the mother and forced the mother to feed the babies. That night the teacher took the babies home so she could feed them, and one of them died. When she brought them back to school on Saturday, she told everyone about what had happened and asked what everyone thought had killed the baby. After hearing what we had to say, the teacher couldn't decide whether to take the remaining baby home or not. On Sunday I went to school in the morning to see if the baby was at school and, if so, how it was doing. But the baby, the mother, and the boxes they were in weren't there. On Monday I found out that the teacher had taken the second baby home and that it had died too.

Parents in the School Community

The school "family" relied heavily on the support of parents, especially the mothers, for practical rather than academic concerns. Membership in the PTA involved both giving this support and benefiting from activities organized for members. For example, the PTA used the sporting facilities and the gym for recreation and for physical-fitness programs for parents. Similarly, the parents organized activities for the children on the school grounds at weekends, so when a child felt like playing outside the home, the area which substituted for the garden or the street as a place to meet friends and play games was often in fact the school playground. Parents were rostered for these occasions and asked to commit themselves to supervisory duty, both during weekends and during school holiday periods. Membership in the PTA was voluntary, and in 1992 and 1993 cost ¥2,500 (A$33, US$25) per academic year. This entitled a parent to participate in the socializing activities mentioned above and to receive a regular news sheet relating to PTA activities in the school once a term, besides making a commitment to helping with special events. The PTA also organized community projects on behalf of the school. For example, recycling projects were organized with members manning a booth on Saturday mornings to collect used cans. On the occasion of the official opening of the school after rebuilding in 1992, the PTA scheduled a special piano recital by professional pianists for the PTA members to enjoy. The PTA also conducted surveys about issues in the school. When the second Saturday of the month was made a school holiday on a trial basis in 1992, a survey of parents and children was immediately conducted to study the effects.

To keep parents and pupils informed, each grade put out its own newsletter regularly, about once each term. The newsletter usually began with a general message from the grade teachers, who wished everybody a successful and happy term and enjoined them to put in their best study efforts. There was always some reference to health, particularly related to the season. So, for example, at the begin-

ning of first term in April, there would be some reference
to the hay-fever period, the pollen count, and whether it
was advisable for hay-fever sufferers to wear a mask or not.
In the winter months, when colds were widespread, children were advised to wash their hands and gargle frequently. The sheet also set out a list of important dates for
meetings and any special excursions for the term. An outline of the topics to be covered in each school subject was
given, allowing parents to judge exactly how much of the
curriculum needed to be covered. This, of course, is of particular importance to many Japanese parents because the
curriculum must be completed to prepare for the exams—
the milestones toward the ultimate university entrance
exam. Sometimes a particular piece of class business, such
as accounting for excursion money, would also be explained.

Ward Participation

The ward office functioned as the center of community activities for the ward, and each school community within
the ward came under its supervision. The school children
received notices from the ward office of holiday programs
and activities, organized and funded by the ward. Most of
the activities were free of charge. Special swimming
lessons, for example, were given during the summer vacation. Team practices and outings took place during the
holidays. Children were advised where they could ride
their bikes safely, and where they should exercise caution
on the roads. When every second Saturday in the month
became a school holiday, parents also received monthly
suggestions about activities available to interest children
in the four hours that they would previously have spent at
school that Saturday.

Our community and school, Honmura, had taken its name from the village that had originally stood on that site, and the community members were very proud of it. A special baseball club, which participated in the competition among teams from our ward, had been formed for the children under the same name. Children interested in playing baseball could enter from the first grade, and there were several levels. The most junior level was made up of students from first to fourth grade. From there you proceeded to the senior primary school section, made up of fifth and sixth graders, and then to the junior high school team. Being a member of the baseball team required tremendous dedication. Practices were held on Wednesdays and Saturdays after school and games were on Sundays from April to December. From December to the end of March, activities were organized to bond the team spirit. So, for example, the children went on excursions such as skiing, exercised to keep in good physical condition for the next season, and sumo wrestled together. There were also special activities for the parents of team members to promote spirit, so with Andy being a member, on occasion I was invited to play softball with the mothers, to go on a family ski trip, to play in a golf tournament, and to go out for an evening of karaoke with other parents.

Nurturing Members in Special Situations

In the school-as-community, children were taught appropriate rituals associated with nurturing members in special situations. Sadly, in Andy's sixth grade, in October 1993, one of his friends lost his mother after a long illness, and the children participated in his grief, as Andy recounted:

A: There's this boy in my class, and his mum had been in the hospital about two months; then she'd come out and she'd been perfectly *genki* (healthy) until about a week before, but then she didn't come to the parents' meeting, according to the teacher. And then one morning the teacher said "*Taihen, taihen, taihen*" [terrible] at the morning sports meeting at about 8:00. Then at the morning meeting she told us that the boy's mum had died.

Q: How did she tell you?

A: Oh, she sat down ... and everybody thought that she was going to tell off the class troublemaker again because he's always getting told off.

Q: And when she's going to tell you off, does she always sit down?

A: Yes, when it's serious ... when it's bad. I mean if it's just something little, well okay, but say if you swore at a teacher, then she would sit down to talk to the whole class.

Q: So does the fact of sitting down mean it's a more serious matter?

A: Yes, and you can tell by her face ... and then she said "*Honda-kun no okāsan ga nakunarimashita* [Honda's mother died], and her eyes went red when she was talking about it, and we were all saying that she [the mother] was so *genki* [active] and everything.

Q: And then what happened after she told you? Did the children ask questions?

A: No, they just said "Ehhhhhhhhh" [a typical Japanese expression of surprise]. And then the teacher went on to talk about it, saying that some people can be so *genki* and then for example a vein in your brain just goes and then you can just die and what a pity and stuff like that. And then it was *zukō* [art] that day and so we had to go there and everybody was talking about funerals and what happens and stuff.

Q: Had some children already been to funerals then?

A: Yes, or some had read about it in a book. Then after art and music we talked about would it be better if we went to the funeral, or would it be better not to because our friend might not want us there, and—you know, it's difficult.

Q: Who talked about it ... all the children with the teacher?

A: Yes, so it's like a class meeting. And we decided that for the *otsuya* [the wake], which I'll explain about in a minute....

Q: Just a minute, in the class meeting did the children make comments and things as well as the teacher?

A: Of course. "I think everybody should go; I think we'd better not go; I think only people who want to go should go." So for the *otsuya*, which is at 7 o'clock at night, we decided people who wanted to should go, and for the funeral also people who wanted to should go, but for the funeral everybody ended up saying they wanted to go. So for the *otsuya* we met in front of the school and then we went up to the *otsuya* place, and on the way the teacher bought a special envelope that you put money in, to give. Then we went there and it had already started.... We all wore dull clothes ... we went to the meeting hall of our area there. And there was incense in little crumbs and you had to pick it up, just a little bit, and put it on your forehead, and there was this rectangular ash-burning thing and you had to put it there. You had to do that three times.

Q: What was the purpose of that?

A: Respect for his mother. And then we got this special stuff—well, there was a box with a handkerchief and a poem card and some special salt which we were given. When you come home into your *genkan* [entrance hall] you are supposed to sprinkle it over your shoulder and this is supposed to stop the spirit coming in with you into your own home. I don't know the whole thing because the adults went in after that. We just waited around until our friend came out of the praying place. See, when we were taking the incense, that was in the back part of the room, but the adults were in the front room chanting this really long religious thing toward the photo of the mother. So we waited until that praying was over and our friend came out, and we said hello and asked if he was okay and he said he was fine, and we went home. Some adults were still there, and their package was supposed to contain saké.

Q: And did you all give money?

A: No, not the kids. Just the adults. Just the teacher as far as I know. I guess some of the adults did later.

Q: But didn't we all contribute ¥400 for something?

A: Oh, maybe that was it.

Q: So it wasn't a very sad occasion then?

A: No, neither was the funeral as far as we saw. For the funeral, we went at about five to one, just in time to see them go off in the carriage.

Q: So the funeral was over really?

A: Yes, all the formal stuff.

Q: The whole class went there?

A: Yes.

Q: And that's all you saw ... the carriage?

A: Yes, it was sort of like a tilly [utility truck] like uncle has on his property in Australia. The back's open and then it had a shrine, like a mini-shrine on it which opened up, and they put the body in there. Then they drove off to have it burnt, and then they collect the bones and worship them for a few days, I think.

Q: What did you feel about the funeral?

A: Well, I couldn't feel too much because all we did was go there and say hi to our friend just before the carriage went off, and see it go off ... with the buses behind so I can't really tell you much about the funeral and I can only tell you a bit about the *otsuya*.

Q: So they didn't really let the children participate in the whole affair?

A: Well, we couldn't in the other part of the *otsuya* because it was like *osake* and things, and we didn't have an invitation. We were just going because he's our classmate, and it's not like we had the invitation to go on the bus. See, when they were leaving, first went the shrine, then went a car, a Toyota Royal Saloon, and in that was the boy and his father, and then behind that two buses of, I think, the special invited people. They were going to the burning with them, I think.

The children were taught to work through the problem as a group, with their main focus being solidarity toward their classmate as a group member.

In fostering community spirit, it seemed that special nurturing and care were also important for the group, and indeed a period was set aside in the timetable for this. For the class, this period was on Saturday.

Q: Andy, on Saturday, there's a period called "Everybody's time." Can you explain what happens then?

A: Well, sometimes we study. Sometimes, say if somebody's leaving—we don't do this much of course, because not everybody leaves all the time—we do an *owakarekai* [goodbye party].

Q: And what happens in that?

A: Well actually, I had one. It was really funny—they thought I was leaving from Saturdays but then I moved in full-time.

Q: Well, what happens at that?

A: Oh, they sing a song, and they play a game. The person who's leaving has to make a speech, and then they all give you a goodbye card.

Q: You mean with everyone's signature on it?

A: No, everybody makes one.

Q: And when do they make it?

A: At home. Oh, I think there's probably one period at school [for it].

Q: OK, well, if nobody's leaving, then what do you do in "Everybody's time"?

A: Well, sometimes we just play. Not too many times though.

A similar period was set aside for the entire school on Thursday:

Q: And then on Thursday there seems to be some kind

of school group activity before the morning meeting?

A: Oh that's called a *shūkai iinkai*. The members of that school group run a meeting: sometimes its a game meeting, sometimes it's a birthday meeting for people with a birthday that month. Sometimes it's an *iinkai happyō*, the announcements of the school groups.

We were also very impressed with the simple but caring way the sixth-grade children prepared Andy's farewell party in January 1994. Three of the children were elected as organizers, and everybody seemed to participate in some way. Under the guidance of the teacher and the organizers, the children baked some sponge cake in the home science facilities and rolled them with strawberries and cream. They prepared a scroll on which each child in the class wrote a personal message to Andy. On Andy's last afternoon, an afternoon tea party was given, entirely run by the children who had been elected organizers. An appropriate speech was made by one of the girls and the scroll was presented. Some special games had been organized by the children, after which they took much delight in sharing the cake they had made. The teacher's role was as a guest, and she did not seem to do anything toward the organization. I noted how unostentatious and delightfully simple the whole affair was.

ENDURANCE IN DIFFICULT SITUATIONS

Expectations in the Japanese system were that children would learn to tolerate situations with patience and would endure quite difficult physical conditions without complaining. I was often surprised at how much was expected of them in this regard.

Whenever there were public holidays, the baseball team took full advantage of them. Extra practices were scheduled, and there was usually a game each day. This happened over the Golden Week holiday period, from 2–5 May 1993, and as Andy describes, very little adjustment was made to the program for inclement weather:

> *Today baseball was from 8:30 in the morning. We practiced until about 10:45 and then went to the game. After the game, because we lost (5 to 1), we had to practice afterwards. It started getting cold and drizzly about halfway through the practice, but we kept on practicing. Finally, when practice finished, our team was wet, cold, and dirty (we had been sliding and the dirt on our uniforms and bodies was running in the rain). We went to eat lunch in the cold rain under a tree, which didn't provide much protection from the rain, and suffered until 3:00. We had to wait until the coaches finished eating, when we were finally allowed to go home. The first thing I did was to have a boiling hot bath and drink some hot tea!*

I have described the great detail that went into caring for the body and its functions in the school, but often these same features seemed to be neglected in the interest of endurance, particularly with the sports teams. When children on the baseball team were cold or hungry or tired, no consideration seemed to be given for their well-being. It was not at all unusual for them to practice or play a game in the rain and cold, and they were always required to wait until they were given permission before having something to eat or drink. One Sunday, for example, they practiced from 10:00 A.M. after having had break-

fast, and then were not allowed to eat before their game at
1:30. The game was delayed until 2:00, so it finished at
3:00, and even then they had to listen to their lecture from
the head coach before they were allowed to eat!

There are many words in the Japanese vocabulary
which reinforce the concept of endurance and persever-
ance: *gambaru* (to do one's best) and *gaman* (bear, endure)
are two of these. I remember one day meeting Andy after
work and school in a busy shopping area of Tokyo to buy
a few things. I had been very busy at work and had an
awful headache, and mentioned this as we were walking
along. Andy quickly retorted unsympathetically, "Just
gaman, Mum!" (Grin and bear it).

I'm not quite sure whether the following episode
should be mentioned as an example of endurance, as it
seems to cross a number of values, but I include it here because of the interpretation given to me afterwards by
Japanese friends who described how heroes in Japan are
those who can endure and persevere, especially against superior physical strength. The episode occurred fairly early
in our full-time commitment to the Japanese system, and
thus at a time when adjusting to some of the different values was somewhat traumatic. It is described in an entry
from my diary of December 17, 1992.

> *This is about the fourth problem we've had in the last two*
> *weeks, and I am really wondering at this stage whether I*
> *shouldn't give up and let Andy go to Singapore to some*
> *other school because it's so hard on him. The cause of this*
> *incident was that last Sunday an unfortunate episode hap-*
> *pened after the baseball practice game. I did not usually at-*
> *tend practice games, but I had to go up to the baseball*

ground and pay some money, so I was there and I witnessed this whole incident. One of the coaches was trying to
get the boys to wrestle ... to sumo wrestle against each other.
Andy is one of the biggest boys in the team and by far the
strongest, I think. This particular coach was very cruel to
them, and he made Andy wrestle three or four times without a break whereas the other children had a break. When
Andy lay flat on the ground exhausted afterwards, the
coach actually jumped on his back, which I was horrified
about. I felt like rushing onto the field to protest, but of
course I couldn't do that, since it would have jeopardized
the child's position. So I did nothing. I just watched. Finally, instead of pitting Andy against bigger boys, he was
put against a small boy from the fourth grade. I was standing next to the boy's mother and let out a gasp of concern,
but she indicated that we had to let it go on and not to
worry. Of course, the inevitable happened and the boy's
arm was twisted and when he cried out in pain, the coach
just moved his arm in many directions and told him he
would be okay. Well, today being Thursday, it seems that
the boy has come back to school with his arm in a sling;
whether it's broken or just sprained I'm not sure, but the
whole school's in a buzz about it. The boy has told everybody that Andy broke his arm on purpose. It seems that
they had a teachers' meeting about it and then Andy's
teacher called him after class, while the others went to art,
and asked him what had happened and whether he had
done it on purpose. It seems that she is trying to find out
what went on, but I have a very sad little boy here at home
tonight, and I really feel quite concerned because I feel it's
the coach's responsibility as an adult to control how the
children play with each other. I have spent all evening

preparing a letter in what I think is appropriate Japanese communication style, to send to the teacher tomorrow expressing my concern. [Later.] After the teacher received my letter, a further meeting was held with the teachers and the nurse, and it was decided that Andy had not done it intentionally. I received a nice note from the teacher telling me this, with the report card a few days later, when the Christmas holiday period began. I had, however, been very concerned with the difference in values and had mentioned the episode to some Japanese friends. The husband, after much thought, explained to me that if you think about it, in Japanese sports there are no classifications by weight. So, for example, in boxing in western countries we use featherweight and heavyweight and so on, whereas in Japanese sports they do not. He suggested that this is because in Japan it is considered extremely good, even excellent, if the smaller person can defeat the bigger one, and it is a question of trying to use your mind to give you your physical force. So for example, in sumo at the moment, a wrestler called Mainoumi excites the crowds no end when he wins, because he is so much smaller than the other wrestlers. I am told that there was another very famous wrestler in Japan whose fame also rested on the fact that he was able to defeat any of the bigger wrestlers despite being very small.

One interesting aspect of our sumo episode among the baseball boys was that the parents let the boy go from Sunday to Wednesday before they took him to the doctor to have his arm checked. Another is, of course, the fact that no mother intervened in the coach's decision, despite the fact that everyone on the side-line appeared concerned about what he was doing.

KNOWLEDGE OF APPROPRIATE COMMUNICATION PATTERNS

There appeared to be some communication strategies operating among the Japanese people which I had not discerned in other cultural groups. The values underlying the rigid socializing skills were also reflected in language patterns. One became extremely conscious of appropriate formulaic structures, perfection in communication, vagueness of expression, and language choice in relation to context and the person with whom one was conversing. The whole focus of communication seemed to be on estimating the feelings of the interlocutor so as to direct the communication towards a harmonious and comfortable conclusion for both parties.

Within any group in Japanese society, there is an acceptable organization based on hierarchical structure, and a consequent recognized order of communication which must be followed, even among children. This was demonstrated when Andy tried to organize Japanese players for a baseball game against some children from his old international school. One of the American mothers from the international school had phoned me seeking advice as to how her children could get to know more Japanese children. One of the things I had suggested was getting the children together for sports or music, or a common theme, and mixing the children on the same teams, rather than having the more usual scenario of a Japanese team against a foreign team. The American mother followed up this suggestion and booked the local baseball field and asked Andy to bring eight of his friends to join the foreigners in playing there.

When Andy phoned round to his Japanese friends, the interaction among the children was most interesting. The first mistake he made was that he did not phone the group leader first, and therefore the first child he phoned said he wouldn't come unless the leader did. The leader's telephone happened to be continuously engaged, and since the others all wanted to know if he was going, it took some time to organize. Andy was able to get four sixth graders besides himself to go, but needed more players to make up numbers. From among the group of fifth graders on the Japanese baseball team, he selected two, but was later reprimanded by the other sixth graders for his choices. A particularly important fifth grader had been ignored.

In any situation of conflict, one of the most important communication patterns for Japanese was the apology. The apology served to conclude the episode harmoniously, no matter how grave that situation might have been, by taking responsibility in a way that seemed to wipe the slate clean and allow the participants to start afresh. When children fought with each other, insulted each other, held up the class or caused the class to miss out on some special treat, an apology was always warranted and made.

I don't know whether or not it was because we were foreigners, but an enormous amount of knowledge was assumed to be self-evident and was never explained. This applied particularly to procedures. When Andy wanted to join the baseball team, knowing that other boys in his class were involved, no one was forthcoming as to how this could be done. After some weeks of questioning, and the help of one mother who seemed to take a liking to us, we were able to learn the ropes. It appeared that it was a matter of predicting what questions to ask in order to lead you to the information you needed. However, when you didn't know the general logic behind procedures, it was often difficult to hit upon the question which would lead you to the appropriate path. An example of this was Andy's new baseball shoes. At the end of September, Andy began complaining that his baseball shoes were too small. New shoes had to be ordered through the team captain's mother, who was automatically the team organizer. We asked her to order the new shoes, but she didn't tell us that the next week was the last game of the season. I thus purchased brand-new shoes for one game!

Complaints were not made openly by the children, but in indirect ways. At the Saturday class meeting, complaints which had been anonymously written on pieces of paper and placed in a box were discussed with the whole class. These ranged from things happening at school to things in the community outside. One child, for example, complained at one session that people were teasing his dog. It appeared that he was extremely attached to his dog, which he regularly took for walks. However, he had named his dog something remarkably similar in pronunciation to the word for a pervert, and all the children who met him during his walks with his dog would tease him by calling the dog a pervert. The boy put an anonymous piece of paper in the complaints box, saying that personal pets should not be teased. This was discussed in class as a general plea for people not to tease dogs; of course, although the complaint was anonymous, effectively everyone knew where it had originated.

Primary-school children in Japan did not enjoy talking to adults, especially foreign ones. One Saturday afternoon

I had to return to my office at the university to collect some materials I had forgotten. When I boarded the train, one of Andy's closest friends, whom I had taken with Andy to the baseball game as a birthday treat, boarded the train in the same carriage. In my usual style I chatted with him in my bad Japanese about where he was going and how long he would be there and other general topics. The boy, who was normally quite extroverted and even noisy when among peers, absolutely froze at having to converse with me and was clearly very embarrassed. I had noticed the same phenomenon with other children in Andy's class, and although in part it was related to age rather than culture, as Andy explained later, it was very difficult for children who were used to conversing on a daily basis in very casual language to converse with an adult, since it required so much attention to polite forms and related changes in the Japanese language itself. Andy felt that the children did not enjoy conversing with adults outside their immediate families for these reasons. Furthermore, Japanese children expected all adults to be fluent in the Japanese language, and I suspect he was also embarrassed that I should lose face using my far-from-perfect Japanese.

Chapter 5

Dealing With Difference

In our experience with the Japanese primary school, we were always at a loss to explain the attitudes toward ostracized members of the group, children of one Japanese parent, and foreign children. We observed that physically handicapped children were treated wonderfully, but that each of the above three groups could be treated cruelly on occasion. It seems that the Japanese are wont to broadly categorize things as either the same or different. Indeed, usage of "right" and "wrong" is not as common in Japanese as is the word *chigau*, which means "different." People, things, and events are easily distinguishable as being the same or different in a largely homogeneous society, where, until fairly recently, people have looked and behaved relatively similarly. Once something has been singled out as different, an appropriate treatment for it is then acknowledged among the group. Problems seem to arise when some new category emerges, for which treatment has not been agreed upon beforehand.

PHYSICALLY-HANDICAPPED CHILDREN

In the case of handicapped children, the acknowledged treatment seemed to be caring and concern. I often thought that one beautiful aspect of our Japanese primary school was the way the handicapped children were cared for and made to feel part of the school and their grade. During our association with the school there were six handicapped children and, while they were at the school, a special teacher was employed to look after each one. There was a special room with facilities set aside in the school for the handicapped children and their teachers. The children spent part of their day in special lessons and, where appropriate—for example art and music classes—were taken in to join the children in their designated grades. They were always given parts in concerts and public activities, and on sports day ran in the races and participated in the activities with all the other children. I never once saw any child being impatient or cruel to a handicapped child, and indeed was always terribly impressed at how someone in the class would always take them by the hand or help them wherever necessary.

AMONG THE JAPANESE CHILDREN

On the other hand, among the Japanese children, where one child was different for some reason—whether due to weakness or strength didn't seem to matter—treatment was often quite harsh and cruel. I observed several of the weaker children desperate to become part of the group, but completely ostracized for some reason. One of these was a little boy whose father had left his mother, who was bringing him up on her own. The mother and child lived with the grandparents, but the mother was often absent from the house, and the child always looked undernourished and was obviously desperately lonely. The mother used to give him huge sums of money to compensate for his situation, and with this money he used to buy the friendship of other children in the class. He would pay them money to play with him—sometimes as much as ¥10,000 [A$135, US$100].

In any discussion of the group in Japanese society, the concept of *uchi/soto* must be mentioned. *Uchi/soto* is a kind of in-group/out-group concept which I had read about and had assumed pertained to the foreigner being the outsider to the Japanese group. However, in my Tuesday women's conversation group, which was comprised of three Japanese mothers from the school and myself, we discussed the concept at some length. It turned out that one of the Japanese mothers had been forced to withdraw her son from the baseball team for which Andy played. In discussing the group dynamics among the parents and children of the baseball team, I was told that several families had had to take their children off the team because both the children and the parents had been excluded from the group. It was said that in our area there was one clique, a central core, and if you were considered an outsider, then its members would resort to unlimited teasing of the children, ostracism of the parents, and so forth. For example, one of the women in the Tuesday group had married a prominent society figure in the area about eighteen years earlier, she herself being from another prefecture. Their son, I was told, had been completely ostracized by the baseball parent clique and finally withdrew. The women explained that in this case they were not considered part of the group because both my friend and her mother-in-law had married into the area and therefore did not have enough connections. Another Japanese friend explained the phenomenon as part of the *murahachibu* "eight tenths of the village" system. This, she said, was an old practice in which some people for certain reasons were excluded from eight designated community activities on the grounds that they were different in some way from the others. Differences could be either positive or negative. It appears, as the Korean writer O-Young Lee mentions in his 1984 book *Compact Culture* (Kodansha International), that the origin of this system stems from the Edo period (1603–1868). During this time,

> ten events were designated as involving group cooperation: birth, coming of age, marriage, death, memorial services for the dead, fire, flood, sickness, setting off on a journey, and building work. If a particular person did something bad or harmful to the village well-being, cooperation would be denied him for eight of the above (only in the event of death or fire would people help him). This gave rise to the term *mura hachibu*, literally "eight tenths of the village," which nowadays has come to mean "ostracism." This and disinheritance essentially mean chasing out someone who is on the "inside." To the extent that people on the "inside" are close to each other, their feelings of exclusiveness toward those on the "outside" are that much stronger. (p. 173)

RETURNEES AND CHILDREN OF ONE JAPANESE PARENT

Two very unfortunate groups in the classification of society members as being either the same or different are returnees from overseas and those children of one Japanese parent, who are given the infelicitous name "half." These children are difficult to categorize, because of appearance, behavior, or both. Each of these two groups would usually try as hard as they might to meld into the Japanese group, often refusing to acknowledge their second language or indeed their parentage. In general, however, they were not accepted, seemingly because by all appearances they should have been Japanese but did not fall into the distinct category of being absolutely different like the foreigner.

The unreasonably high suicide rate among Japanese youth and the increase in delinquency may also be attributed, at least in part, to exclusion from the group, although this seemed not to manifest itself so much in the primary school age group as it did in junior high school and high school. The son of an American acquaintance, who had recently divorced her Japanese husband, became a delinquent at the age of fourteen, spending his nights in parks, using drugs, missing school, and so on. Apparently he had never been accepted into the groups at his school and had suffered ever since. Degree of acceptance seemed to be related to possibility of categorization, associated status, and physical presence. In a society that admired and emulated the West, a typical WASP child like mine—white, Anglo-Saxon, male, big, and strong—seemed to have a better chance of being accepted than children of other nationalities, for example Iranian or Korean, or than the "halfs."

FOREIGNERS

The Japanese demonstrated peculiar attitudes toward foreigners, who are called *gaijin* in the Japanese language. The two Chinese characters representing the word "*gaijin*" literally mean "outside person," that is, a person outside the Japanese group—but in general foreigners are categorized as different and definitely "strange." However, not all foreigners fall into the same category, and the difference in attitude toward European foreigners, as opposed to Asian foreigners, was quite noticeable. With the former there seemed to be a sort of love/hate relationship—love because Western society was much admired, yet hatred because of some sort of inferiority complex. On the other hand, with Asian and African foreigners a superiority complex prevailed, and these foreigners were often treated with disdain. Overall, foreigners were supposed to look different and behave differently, which brought with it the frustrations of never being able to enter the Japanese group, but some advantages in getting away with things which might otherwise have been unacceptable in Japanese society. For example, the school never coerced me into buying the expensive school bag for Andy that the other children had, and I was not expected to do everything the other mothers did.

Foreigners were often treated as token representations of internationalization, as I suspect would be the interpretation of the following episode described in my diary entry from October 1992.

> Today a very strange thing happened. It was the day of the primary-school bazaar. Mothers had been asked many months before which area they would like to work in, and I had volunteered for the drinks stand. We had had several

meetings about that, and I was fairly useless to the other mothers over those meetings because I couldn't speak well enough in Japanese to help them decide what drinks to buy. I didn't have a car to be able to go and get drinks either, and I didn't have a big refrigerator to be able to make lots of ice for them. However, they asked me if I would dress in a kimono and serve on the stand, and I consented. A try-on of the kimono was held about a month before. On the day of the bazaar, I was due to go up to the school at 8:00 in the morning to help set up, put on the kimono, and then wear it during the course of events. Well, of course, I imagined that all the other mothers were wearing their kimonos too, but as it turned out only one other mother was wearing one. There were two sections to the drinks stand: one where they sold soft drinks and the other where they served tea—that is, ocha *[Japanese tea] with* okashi *(in this case, special bean-paste cakes) such as they would serve in a tea ceremony. There were all sorts of giggles about me serving on the stand in the first place, and shortly before I put the kimono on I suggested that perhaps I shouldn't do so because it was a Japanese thing and therefore would not be appropriate for a foreigner. They then explained to me through one woman who spoke English that to them it was like the Miss World contest, and it would make their booth very important if they had a celebrity attraction like a foreigner dressed in a kimono serving the tea. Somewhat curious as to what this might exactly mean, I consented to do it and was helped into my kimono. When I was ready in my straitjacket, I found that the two teachers running the stand were actually the special education teachers who were in charge of the handicapped children, and that the handicapped children were serving in this tea ceremony too. So*

*all in all there were three retarded children, myself, two
young girls who had been brought in to help, and the three
special education teachers, two of whom were also wearing
kimonos. I spent a very long day as the curiosity piece for
the tea ceremony stand, after which I had sore leg muscles
for at least a week in consequence of the excessive deferential
bows one must learn to make in offering the tea to guests in
traditional tea ceremony style.*

Foreigners were very often treated as curiosity pieces
in this way. In one of my intercultural communication
classes at the university, students were asked to present
what they thought to be a symbol of Japanese culture, and
one of my best students and his group presented Japanese
humor. This particular student had been away from Japan
for five years, and one of the things that stunned him on
his return was that the Japanese loved to ridicule foreigners, especially celebrity foreigners. They put them on television, for example, and subjected them to all sorts of
somewhat humiliating jokes like spraying them with foam.
Under normal circumstances the foreigners involved
would have found this unacceptable, but since they were
paid big money they endured it. However, the Japanese
were really ridiculing the foreigners, finding this sort of
activity especially humorous.

Andy experienced this "special" treatment as a foreigner
all the time. The following is his description of one such
instance at the Suzuki concert. This concert was held every
year in March in Tokyo, with approximately 3,000 children participating. The concert hall was enormous, and
the children performed on a central circular stage, from
the perimeter of which tiers of seats were constructed up-

ward toward the roof dome. The children were organized to walk into the bowl at the appropriate time by the number of the piece they were playing, and this organization took place in the tunnels underneath the seats.

Today was the Suzuki National Concert. Mum and I went with an American family from my violin class, who have three boys doing Suzuki violin. Out of the three, the eldest was qualified to play. The other two kids came to the concert just to listen. When we got there, I went to the students' seats to wait for my dreaded walk down the stairs to the concert space. I dread it because it is such a long procedure. On the way to the middle part of the Budokan [hall], all the kids were staring at me. I wasn't very mad because I am used to being stared at and discriminated against. But my friend was pretty mad and, being a first-timer in the discriminating business, made faces back at the Japanese kids who were staring at him (exactly what they want you to do—more things to tease you about). So they started staring at him more and more. Back in my section, I was getting madder and madder at the Japanese kids, but, luckily, before I lost my temper and got into a fight, the violin part of the concert started for me. After the concert had finished, my friend and I were in one of the most inside rows (meaning one of the last to get out) and while we were waiting, we were being stared at by the other Japanese kids. I had had about enough of them calling me "Bakagaijin" [stupid foreigner] and asked my friend if he had. Just as I thought, he had. So I put on the old rushing, studying-hard, cute-little-kid act and told one of the teachers that I had to do something and had to go out early. Well, that's it. He let me out. A happy ending.

Foreigners were expected to have strange ideas about things too, especially where something considered to be Japanese was concerned. I must admit that Andy did become disheartened at times, and these were usually when he became fed up with being the odd man out because he was the foreigner. One of these times was in cooking class. The children were put into groups of five on a Friday, in preparation for making a vegetable dish in the Saturday morning cooking class. The group needed to arrange the timing, buy the ingredients, and decide how they were going to organize things. At one stage a discussion arose about the timing for cooking broccoli, and the other children all agreed that fifteen minutes were needed to steam broccoli. Andy was sure that not more than a few minutes would be needed and said so. Because the Japanese children had all agreed and Andy's was the only different opinion, this was thought to be the foreigner's way of cooking broccoli. After the teacher's intervention, the shorter time was agreed upon, but nevertheless, on the Saturday when they did cook the vegetables, they were eaten cold as is the case more often than not in Japan, and the Japanese children thought it quite strange that Andy preferred to eat them hot.

The children also seemed to find foreign teachers a source of amusement, and they did not receive the respect that was assigned to a Japanese teacher. Our ward, Minato ward, is very much intent upon internationalizing the school curriculum, and one of the ways it endeavors to do so is by occasionally sending foreign teachers to the primary schools. The following is Andy's description of this procedure:

Q: How often do the foreign teachers come into your classroom?

A: I've only seen three so far, so maybe twice a year. There have been two in sixth grade. But when they come they go round the whole school and visit every class. They all teach in English, and then they teach different things, like about their country.

Q: What is the attitude of the children to these foreign teachers?

A: I think they enjoy them, but I don't think they take them too seriously.

Q: Don't they? What makes you think that?

A: Well, first of all they laugh all the time. The foreign teachers ... you know, the accent and stuff is just kind of funny.

Q: What, when they speak Japanese?

A: Well, they can't speak their own language in the class although they do say things like, "This is 'hello' in German" or English or whatever. For example, one walked into the class and put his hands up and said in a loud voice "I am X [name]," and then shouted it again even louder. Then he wrote his name on the board with an exclamation mark on the end. And then one boy asked "What's the bat for?" meaning that the exclamation mark looked like a baseball bat. And then he taught us about Denmark. And it was really funny because he'd just been teaching a second-grade class, and he hadn't rewound the video, and he kept on asking us *"Chotto matte kudasai"* [Wait a moment] over and over again with this funny accent.

Q: Well, then, did the children enjoy the lesson?

A: Oh, I think so; they were laughing all through it, and I was too.

We both felt that when Japanese children were negative in their behavior toward foreigners, in many cases their attitude had been influenced by the views of their parents and older brothers and sisters. The following is a conversation I had with Andy in this regard:

Q: Remember that one night when we were walking up the street and a third grader and his parents came down the hill and he just ignored you and pretended you didn't exist?

A: Oh, the kids do it sometimes.

Q: Why do you think they do that?

A: I guess because some of the mothers say, "Stay away from gaijins." I mean it happened the other day too. There was this second grader who I quite like, and I asked him if he was going to the Kumon.... He answered Sannohashi [a place name], and his *oniisan* [older brother] said, "*Mushi, mushi*" [Ignore him, ignore him], so it's influence from the older ones; that *oniisan* is in fifth grade in my school but I hadn't done anything to him. So I think it's influence from the mothers or fathers or older brothers and sisters.

Q: It's sad for them, though, don't you think?

A: It's kind of sad for me, too. It's sure hard to make friends.

Ostracism

The hardest thing for Andy in being the foreigner was that he was left out of groups more often than not. There were many incidents in which Andy suffered in this regard. For example, he was often left out of organized activities. When you joined a team in the Japanese system it was an all-or-nothing commitment; so even in the off-season, all kinds of activities were organized for the baseball team members to participate in. On Sundays in the off-season, team members went off and did other things together. On one occasion, when the boys did sumo wrestling, Andy arrived at the appointed place to find that his name hadn't been put on the list by the mothers and so he wasn't able to participate. They just left him off and said that he could play next year. Well, at first I was irate. My immediate thought was that it was another case of the foreigner being left out, a complex one tends to develop after a while. However, trying to look at the situation objectively a little later on, I decided that there could have been a number of reasons for their behavior. Perhaps they thought that he might be hurt; often their attitude seemed to be that, because we were foreigners, we could not possibly do anything Japanese. Perhaps they simply thought that he wouldn't want to participate. It was impossible to know, as the major difficulty with operating in Japanese society is that often things are not made explicit. But it did often seem that he was left out.

Further incidents relating to ostracism from the group are related by Andy himself:

> *September 1992*
>
>   *At baseball when it rains or has rained and we cannot use the field, we go to a place called* kōsokushita. *Kōsoku-shita means an area below the raised expressway, so it is dry.*[11]
>
>   *One day when we had training at* kōsokushita, *the guys on the team wouldn't throw the ball to me. I kept raising my glove ready to catch but they would only throw*

the ball to me one in fifty times. The only balls I could get were the ones that the batter hit to me (there was a pitcher, pitching to a batter).

For me it was a mini-war. For them it was just a "leave out the foreigner" game. What's more, they were winning by a hundred points to one.

I was feeling down. I kept missing the ball and then kept getting angry about it. When it came my turn to bat, I was so angry that out of about ten pitches I got six hits and two home-runs!

On Thursday the 17th of September, ichikumi [first class] and nikumi [second class] of my grade decided that that day would be a good time to take the class photo.

This year, since we got additional space in the school photo book—two pages—we decided to break up into groups and take photos so that the people looking at the book could see our faces larger. We had to make a choice in our groups of whether we wanted the picture taken on the roof, in the classroom, or in the playground.

After the teacher had finished explaining this, she told us to make five groups of four and one group of five among the boys, and five groups of four and one group of six among the girls. I decided just to wait and see who were my friends by which people let me in their group.

When the groups were chosen and nobody had asked me to join their group, I realized that three groups of six and one group of five had been formed, so that a guy in the class who is not well liked and I were the only ones left out.

I kept telling the teacher, but she was too busy taking the girls' pictures so she couldn't talk. Finally she finished and we were told to come to her and listen. Everybody came except the other boy who had been left out. He was so *mad that nobody wanted him in their group that he was throwing a ball against the wall with all the strength he had. (I felt like doing it too, but if they know you feel like that, they just tease you more.)*

It took all the boys to stop him, and bring him to the group. The teacher then told us that it was supposed to be groups of four, four, four, four, and six and to do it that way. We did it that way and finally we got the groups right and took our photos.

The bad thing was that I was so upset I looked bad for the photo!

October 1992

One Saturday when it was a holiday from school, there was a sports festival that was hosted by the baseball teams in my league. My team was one of the three teams that lead the different sports groups into a sort of ring. By this time the coaches were beginning to like me, so I was one of the eleven to lead in the different sports groups.

We waited until all the sports groups had lined up behind signs marking their sports. At nine o'clock, when everybody was lined up in front of the signs, we went into the ring, circled around, and lined up in the center. Then the sports groups handed back some large trophies in exchange for little ones, to show that they had won the large ones.

After that, about thirty people made speeches saying practically the same thing each time. Every speech started out with, "Good morning everyone," and then "The weather is very good, isn't it? There's not a cloud in the sky."

After all the speeches, the kantoku [head coach], who is

*kind to others, volunteered us to help clean up. After we
had stored all the trophies that were handed back in a
room, we were told that we were free to go around in
groups to eat and play. I went around asking at least one
person from each group if I could join them. All of them
said no. I was wandering off by myself with no one to talk
or eat or play with when I met the team captain by himself
too. "Can I join your group?" I asked him. He asked why
I wasn't with the kids my own age and I explained that
they wouldn't let me in. He said I could join him but that
he wasn't on his own and that he was meant to be with a
friend but he just couldn't find him.*

*For the first half of the day I wandered around with
him, but about halfway through he wandered off and I
couldn't find him. But I met another kid and so I played
with him for the last half.*

*Altogether, after I had found someone to play with, it
was a great day!*

BULLYING

Closely linked to this phenomenon of social categorization is the concept of bullying in Japanese schools, about
which much has been written in the press. Taken in isolation and evaluated from an outsider's point of view, the
bullying phenomenon is extremely alarming. There is a
very fine line between teasing and bullying, and it seems
to me that most of what went on in the Japanese primary
school was closer to teasing than bullying. Andy's comments on what he terms "bullying" are as follows:

*There is quite a lot of bullying at school to the weak kids. I
think that this is half just showing off. I think that they*

bully weaker kids so that they can always win and show off to other kids. But they will not bully the stronger kids because there is a chance of losing. They will also not bully a popular kid because if they do, that kid's friends will come and bully back.

It was not our experience to encounter bullying of the kinds commonly described in the press. Some such incidents, reported in 1993 as having occurred in various parts of Japan over a four-month period, were as follows:

- A fifteen-year-old ninth grader jumped in front of a train in Hokkaido after six months of being beaten in classrooms and forced to shoplift by his peers.
- A seventeen-year-old high-school student in Nagano died in school at the hand of a bully with a knife.
- A fourteen-year-old boy died in Okinawa a day after nine schoolmates beat him for threatening to report their bullying.
- A thirteen-year-old boy hanged himself in the sports activity room of a school in Tochigi Prefecture after he had broken down and cried when schoolmates, who had been ganging up on him for months, repeatedly forced him to be "it" in a mock game of blindman's bluff.

These incidents all involved junior-high and high-school students and not primary-school students, so perhaps bullying is associated with the increase in pressure as the students move toward the entrance exam and encounter increasingly stressful study requirements.

Because the bullying situation had become so critical, officials were forced to take some steps toward improving the situation, and in 1993 it was reported that 14,000 special social workers would be employed to work with children in the schools. Certainly, many of the Japanese people we knew were concerned not only about the Japanese children but also about the bullying of foreigners in Japanese schools. An incident which occurred in February 1993 describes the almost excessive concern on the part of some local friends for Andy's position in the Japanese school. My diary describes the events:

> Andy came home from school and said, "What is your friend Satoko's last name?" I said it was Mitsukoshi, and he asked what her name was before she was married. I said I didn't know and asked why he wanted to know. He said "Well, I'm not allowed to tell you. The teacher has told me not to tell you." At this point I got extremely angry, as the teacher's request was interfering in communication between my son and me. I coerced him into telling me what had happened, and he proceeded to tell me that the school had received a letter from a person called Okuna who lived in a reasonably nearby part of Tokyo—Yoyogi or maybe Shibuya. The letter had indicated that its author knew that Andy was a victim of bullying and teasing at school and that the school should do something about it. Andy had been called in by the vice-principal, who had asked him whether he was unhappy. When I heard, I couldn't imagine who of my friends would send such a letter and rather resented the interference, though I recognized its intention as well-meaning.
>
> That night I went down to my usual Friday evening conversation meeting at the Mitsukoshi's. The Mitsukoshi family had a lot of anger stored up inside them toward

Japanese society. Theirs was a typical story of a Japanese family sent abroad by the husband's company, only to return and find their child bullied unmercifully by the Japanese children because he no longer fitted into the group. When I arrived there, I asked Satoko what her name was before she was married and she replied that it was Okuna. I asked her where her parents lived and she told me that they lived in Yoyogi. I then asked her if she had by chance sent a letter to Andy's school and she, too, was astounded at the thought. Then a wave of possible recognition came across her face, and she hinted that she might know who had. She immediately made a call to her mother, and it turned out that her mother had been following all the stories that we had been discussing on Friday nights in our conversation group through her daughter and had taken particular note of those referring to Andy's adaptation to the school. She had taken it upon herself to send a letter to the school saying that she knew neither Andy nor his mother, but that she had heard from other people that we were having a hard time because Andy was being bullied at school. She said in the letter that, in the interests of Japan's internationalization and being kind to foreigners, she felt they should look into the matter. She gave the school her name and address and telephone number and the vice-principal in fact followed up by telephoning her. On that occasion he told her that he would look into it. He said that he was completely unaware that Andy was having a hard time and that, although he couldn't communicate well with me, he felt that I was comfortable in the school environment, as I seemed to be relaxed with the PTA and school activities. My friend's mother insisted in that phone call that she wanted him to take immediate action and was quite forceful in her approach, something fairly unnatural for a Japanese woman in dealing with a teacher. The whole intervention was most extraordinary, as well as being unfounded, and on reflection I felt that it could only be explained by the absolute anger of this woman, whose own grandchild had been bullied and victimized by Japanese society so badly when he returned to primary school in Japan, after having spent some years in Spain, that the family was forced to withdraw him. They had chosen to put him in a boarding school in Britain rather than have him bullied in Japan. The grandmother was apparently determined that other children would not suffer in the same way.

Chapter 6

Feedback

PERFORMANCE

A school report card was sent home at the end of each term (three times in each academic year), and parents were required to sign it and write comments if they so desired. It was extremely detailed and interesting both for its content and for the way students were graded. The first page was dedicated to "school life" in four sections: personal characteristics (followed by teacher's comments), special activities (followed by teacher's comments), attendance, and a section where parents could comment.

The characteristics were listed with explanations as follows:

Characteristics	Explanation
Independence, perseverance	Makes a plan and makes an effort to complete it
Responsibility	Knows his job (committee) at school and can do it

Originality, imagination	Devises new ideas to improve school life
Consideration	Is conscious of gratitude to others, is kind to people and empathizes with them
Service	Knows importance of working for others and volunteers
Public spirit and fairness	Empathizes with others and acts with fairness.

Each child was graded for each term either with a circle which meant "good" or nothing, which meant "normal." Interestingly, Andy's "good" marks were in originality/ imagination, consideration, and public spirit/fairness. Comments by the teacher regarding Andy were concerned with his ability to fit into the group and how he handled tasks.

Under "special activities," both the student activity (in fifth grade, the nursing group for Andy) and the club activity (in fifth grade, swimming) were mentioned. Comments followed about performance in these areas.

The attendance report was quite detailed, setting out first the months school was open (every month except August); then the number of possible school days in each month was listed, with the total per year coming to 238 days. (This meant, of course, that there were only 127 days off in a year; and with 52 of those being Sundays and 11 special Saturdays, there were only 64 days of actual vacation, including public holidays.) Next, absences for reasonable excuses were listed. Reasonable excuses included illness and societal commitments such as funerals, memorial services for relatives, and other family commitments recognised as being important. Not much advantage seemed to be taken of the "reasonable excuses" concept, and most children attended school on a regular basis. Finally, absences for no good reason were listed, followed by the number of days attended each month.

The second page of the report card was dedicated to academic records, comments by the teacher, and the signatures or *hanko* of the principal, teacher, and parents. The subjects were listed with four objectives for each subject explained. Alongside each of the four objectives, a double circle (meaning "good"), a circle ("normal"), or a triangle ("needs attention") were drawn. Then an overall grade was given by drawing a circle on one of three steps along a continuum from left to right of "very good," "good," and "try a little harder." The objectives for each subject are translated below:

Japanese
- reads books often and understands them
- speaks and writes competently
- can understand various expressions of thought
- understands basic language structure

Social Studies
- interested in Japanese products, industry, and farming, and tries to study by himself
- understands life and industry in different areas of Japan
- uses data to explain
- understands connection between industry and Japanese life

Math
- number and shape recognition, problem-solving and calculation skills

- logical reasoning and prediction skills
- calculation, measurement, drawing graphs
- basic recognition of amounts and graphs

Science
- keen to study, values living things
- thinks and judges logically, based on facts
- does observations and experiments and can express process and result precisely
- understands natural conditions, weather and other phenomena, and movement of stars and planets

Music
- interested in music, willingly joins musical activities
- can feel the beauty of music, can think up and compose music
- has mastered the basic techniques of musical expression
- shows appreciation for music joyfully and enjoys its richness and beauty

Art
- interested in creating things
- has the imagination to think about the purpose and beauty of creative work
- can make things using creative skill and the sense of forming and shaping things
- enjoys a work of art, its beauty and richness

Home Studies
- has learned about the jobs associated with clothes, food, and home
- can think about life around him and about improving daily life

- has mastered basic techniques with regard to clothes, food, and living
- understands what is desirable in home life

Physical Education
- seeks enjoyment in exercise and is conscious of health and safety
- finds a theme for own exercise
- has mastered the techniques necessary for various sports
- understands the development of the body and the mind and the causes of and protection against injury.

There was no pass/fail system between grades in the Japanese primary school. This meant of course that nobody needed to repeat any year, but nobody could progress faster than the age group either. Andy found that this sometimes caused disruption of the class procedure, when a child did not have the ability to follow the curriculum and constantly distracted everybody else from learning.

In the primary school itself, there were parent-teacher conferences on a one-to-one basis, as well as conferences where the teacher met with the parents as a group. The group conference was held once every term—three times each year. As a general rule, the one-to-one conferences were given three times each year, twice at the school and once in the home. In the conference at school, the procedure seemed fairly similar to any other parent-teacher conference I had attended at other schools. Due to language difficulties, I actually only attended this meeting on one occasion, and that time I was allowed to take in a tape

recorder so as to be able to reflect on comments later. The
parent-teacher conference in the home was a traditional
part of the Japanese education system which seemed to be
fading out of practice with changes in society. Its original
purpose was for the teacher to be able to see in what conditions and under what circumstances the student was
studying. At our school, not everybody chose to have the
home visit from the teacher, and indeed I elected not to
participate. Apparently the encounter was never a very
long one, with the teacher arriving and being offered some
tea, observing the surroundings, and then leaving. However, I suspect that what goes on in the home visit depends very much on the teacher, and perhaps on the area
too. Karen Hill Anton's has given a very interesting description of the home visit in a more rural area of Japan.
It seems that in the country, the elementary school teacher
always makes the home visit once each year and spends
twenty to thirty minutes at each home. On this occasion,
parents are anxious to please the teacher, who is afforded
considerable status in Japanese society, and the teacher is
glad to have the opportunity of meeting parents outside
the school environment. Often the topics of conversation
are not directly related to school, but rather to family and
societal concerns. This time-consuming home visit is in
addition to the teacher's commitments in the classroom.

A similar report, emphasizing the child's overall performance in context, was given to us in 1991, when Andy attended the YMCA camp during the summer holidays. A
detailed report from the camp leader about the child's performance on that occasion was sent home. It showed the
concern and care given in the Japanese system for all aspects of the child's involvement and focused on interac-

tion with other children, overall behavior, health, appetite, and bowel movements.

While achievement formed only part of the primary school focus, achievement formed the basis for the test-taking orientation of the private cram schools. Even in the Kumon cram school, which was considered a moderate example of the breed, the monthly newsletter which was sent home with the invoice listed exam dates, gave the usual words of encouragement to study harder, and reported the percentage pass rate among the students on the tests. Students who were ahead of their level were commended, along with the most outstanding student and the students who were particularly good at either math or Japanese. A consultancy day was set aside for parents to speak with the cram school teachers concerning their child's progress, just like the parent-teacher interviews in the regular school system.

BEHAVIOR

At various times, the mass media in Japan—and the foreign press in particular—has focused on physical violence on the part of teachers in administering discipline in schools. In our experience, there was no such violence in Andy's school, and indeed the school seemed very concerned in this regard. It has also been reported that teachers often lead a class in imposing group punishment upon an errant child. This was never our experience. However, on a number of occasions, we observed them stand by and wait until the violent behavior resolved itself.

Andy had his own view on teachers' punishment of behavioral misdemeanors:

It's really difficult these days. You know, before they used to put you out in the corridor or slap you or something when you did something really bad. That's what our teacher said she used to do. But these days you can't do much because the parents get all upset.

What Japanese teachers seemed to do, and very effectively, was use discussion to focus on the shame the behavior in question would bring both to the individual and to the members of any groups to which he might belong (in the case of the primary school, his school or class). One of the most common ways of disciplining behavior across Japanese society seemed to be the threat of how the others in the group might judge it, sometimes referred to as the "all eyes upon you" approach. This was illustrated further in a postcard I received in 1993 from one of my former Japanese students on a homestay program in Canada, in which she said: "I feel very free here. Every other person looks free. I don't worry about others' eyes here somehow." Andy too felt the "eyes" in discipline. One day when I asked him how his day had been, he said, "Today was pretty tough because the teacher had eyes for me and I don't know why." We later found out some of the other children had complained because Andy had been praised for his good work, particularly in Japanese. It was apparently not considered good to make a foreign child the positive example in studying the Japanese language, so the teacher evidently felt she had to meld him back into the group.

Where blame is concerned, the innocent-until-proven-guilty principle certainly prevailed. Much time was spent hearing both sides of a story and in telling each side where they had erred. Children were urged to accept responsibility through punishment meted out to the whole group. An example of this occurred at the sixth-grade camp in October 1993. On that occasion, one of the nights had been set aside for the children to sleep outdoors in tents, but strict rules with regard to conduct had been imposed. Several of the boys became overexcited and started making too much noise, and a comic book (forbidden on the trip) had been found in one of their tents. In consequence, all the children were called inside and no one was allowed to sleep in the tents.

It was not our experience that teachers in Andy's school regularly abused students, physically or verbally. In fact, the antithesis was usually the norm: a kind and caring attitude geared toward working together in social harmony.

However, on the baseball team some physical punishment was meted out to offenders by the coaches, as described in the following interview.

Q: In the baseball team the coaches still hit and kick the kids, don't they?

A: Yes, when you make lot of errors, or if they tell you to do something and you do it a different way or you can't do it, they get mad.

Q: When they hit you, where do they hit you on your body?

A: Most of them just hit you with the knuckles on the head, but sometimes if the coach is mad at a guy that's really clumsy, he'll kick him. Well, I guess they're aiming for the stomach, but you always turn around so it ends up hitting you on the back.

Although my own view was that such disciplining was potentially very dangerous, the Japanese mothers did not question the authority of the coaches. In the face of such conflicting values, I felt there were only two choices open to me: to pull our child out of the Japanese system, or to accept it, since the Japanese system did not allow parents to contest it openly without some repercussions for the child.

Even on occasions when physical punishment was not given, sometimes I found the verbal reprimands extraordinarily harsh for the offense. When the baseball team lost games, they were really treated with a heavy hand. On one occasion, the captain was severely reprimanded and was made to cry. His personal errors had not been solely responsible for the loss, but it seemed as if the whole team's grief had to be borne by the captain as leader. He seemed to have to accept the punishment for whatever the team had done wrong. On other occasions when the team lost by a small margin—for example 6–5—the *kantoku* (head coach) screamed at them and each coach gave them a lecture afterwards. When they lost very badly—for example 11–1, when the children did nothing right—they were made to bear the shame by being ignored altogether, as if they weren't even worth talking to.

Just as there was punishment, there were also rewards. Rewards in the baseball team required some considerable effort. In the early stages of our association with the baseball team, Andy was missing an emblem from the top of his baseball team uniform. When we inquired where we should purchase it, we were told that he couldn't have that emblem until he had done something for the team to earn it, such as hitting a home run or catching well. After each match, the coaches singled out players who had played exceptionally well, and in order of merit these players were given soft drinks and their meritorious play discussed with the rest of the team.

DISCIPLINE ACROSS CULTURES

Attitudes toward disciplining children in the Japanese system appear to be quite different from those in other countries. When Japanese children and foreign children came together in the same study group, this became quite a problem. One such place was the Kumon private tutoring school which Andy attended twice each week for the whole time we were in Japan. Kumon was run by Japanese, in Japanese style. Younger Japanese children attended, but fewer of the older ones did, since from about the fourth grade specialized cram schools were more popular. Kumon was also frequented in our area by many foreign children whose parents felt that the international schools were not preparing them adequately with the basic skills in mathematics and adequate knowledge of the writing system in Japanese. Most of these foreign children were attending under duress, and found it particularly difficult to cope with Japanese-style teaching, and the small spaces provided for study in a room filled with other children of all ages. The Japanese children tended to be quite unruly at times, and this seemed to be taken by the foreign children as a license to be quite undisciplined themselves. The whole scene often became one of a playground rather than a study location. The Japanese teachers (like those in the primary school) would not discipline the children severely under those circumstances. Rather, they tended to wait until the children had sorted it out for themselves. On the other hand, the expectations of the foreign children were that some sort of direction would come from the Japanese teacher.

Many foreign parents found the situation intolerable and complained, or tried to take the matter into their own hands, as occurred in one incident in which we were involved. On that occasion, in November 1993, Andy returned home from Kumon at 7:00 P.M., absolutely terrified and in tears. (He does not cry easily, nor does he have any fear, especially in Japan.) He described a scene where the father of one of the younger children at Kumon had waited for him outside, accused him of distracting his daughter from her studies, kicked his bike in several places, followed him up the hill where he kicked the bike again, and swore at Andy, saying he would wait for him again if his daughter told him of any more trouble. When I heard the story I was somewhat bewildered, since I had never heard of a Japanese father behaving in this way, so I jumped on my bicycle on that cold and rainy evening and went with Andy to the teachers at the Kumon school, seeking some clarification. The teachers were also amazed, and after further discussion we worked out that the father concerned was not Japanese, and that the child was a student at the international school which Andy had attended prior to moving to the Japanese one. Through my contacts there, it was very easy for me to find the telephone number of the parents, and the Japanese teachers were more than happy for me to deal with a *gaijin* problem rather than having to deal with it themselves. When I sought an explanation from the irate father, it interestingly turned out that he had on at least one other occasion contacted parents of what he considered problem children, seeking to rectify a situation which, in his view, was unacceptable and certainly not conducive to his daughter's learning. The interesting facts of the episode to me were that, first of all, he had entered his daughter in a Kumon class unprepared to accept the process of classroom interaction in Japanese-run schools, and second of all that he should consider it his right to discipline the child of somebody else attending the school. The Japanese teachers were most concerned about his behavior and made a point of telephoning us late that night to make sure that both Andy and I were quite safe in the face of this extreme behavior.

Chapter 7

Reflections

THE JAPANESE PRIMARY SCHOOL EXPERIENCE FOR ANDY

For Andy, the experience of attending the Japanese primary school proved unique and positive—in all, wonderful.

Our original interest in sending him to a Japanese school was to have him learn the language through interacting with Japanese people. Australia is committed politically and economically to being part of Asia, and it had become extremely important for Australian children to be familiar with as many Asian languages and cultures as possible. We felt that if Andy could study Japanese until the end of primary school, he would have learned the two syllabic scripts (*kana*), and the approximately nine hundred Chinese characters around which *kana* are woven. With language inextricably tied to culture, we felt that an understanding of the Chinese characters would not only lead him toward understanding the Japanese people, but might also help him later in learning the Chinese language and understanding other Asian countries with a strong Chinese cultural heritage. However, appreciating the high level of difficulty of the Japanese language, I was conscientious in monitoring his progress; had the whole experience proved too difficult, I would have taken him out, since I had other options for his education at the time. Happily, he learned to love the language and achieved a high standard in his class, emerging from primary school, as his Japanese peers did, with sufficient reading ability to begin reading books other than school textbooks, which in Japan need to be written for the grade level of *kanji* acquisition.

Through learning the language and interacting with Japanese people, we also hoped Andy would learn to understand Japanese people, operate in Japanese society, and make Japanese friends. He achieved all three of these objectives, but never succeeded in achieving membership status. Many times he felt welcome and comfortable, but he was often marginalized and/or treated differently from the other children. In short, he was always a guest. This would seem to be the norm rather than the exception, and many foreigners operating in different age groups have documented similar experiences. During my time in Japan, I cannot remember ever having met a foreigner who actually felt entirely accepted in Japanese society, even though some people I know have spent twenty or thirty years in Japan, often with a Japanese spouse. Even so, Andy built up very solid relationships there, not only with the children in his class but with his teacher, with other children's parents, with his baseball coaches, and with his *senpai* and *kōhai*.

We were also interested in sending Andy to Japanese school to improve his basic skills, particularly in math but also in other areas which require a certain amount of rote memorization. Japanese education placed a lot of emphasis on rote memorization—perhaps too much in the long run—but we felt rote-learning skills, and the associated discipline of the mind, could be very useful in later life. Whether or not he did benefit from the experience in this regard remains to be seen.

Last but not least, we had been very impressed, from our first encounters with Japan, with some of the societal values such as politeness, group interaction, diligence, and commitment to achievement. Operating within a new set of cultural parameters, Andy's behavioral patterns changed quite substantially in some areas. Whereas he had been quick and slapdash in his schoolwork preparation in other schools, the Japanese attention to detail and perfection forced him to focus on presentation, with the result that his written language became reasonably well formed both in Japanese and in English. The focus on health left him very conscious of his weight and height in relation to his peers, and also focused on a balanced diet and exercise. He now also sets high objectives for himself and, when he does not achieve these, tends to be overly self-critical. Undoubtedly he learned a love of the Japanese language and way of life and, with that, an ability to empathize with another person's values.

He enjoys being part of a community and learned to be sensitive enough to the behavior of others to conform where necessary. Through his experience of being one of few foreigners, he became sensitive to the needs of others who are different from the group majority, although I would have to say he learned this the hard way and suffered a lot. He resented being left out of the Japanese groups so often, but did learn that in some societies individual needs are not of prime concern. He was emotionally unable to handle the teasing that came his way, and we spent much time talking about these situations at night to help him deal with them. However, in dealing with the values of a new culture, much depends on individual personality traits, and experiences for Andy in his interactions in the Japanese primary school are quite likely to have been very different from those of other children.

Through operating with more rigid respect forms in both Japanese language and behavior, he became more conscious of politeness, but when he first returned to Australia he sometimes had problems relating appropriate behavior to context. For example, he insisted on looking down when he was being addressed by a master at his new school, instead of making eye contact. The first report card from his new school stressed how very polite he was, so much so that I questioned him as to how this was being manifested. It appeared that because in the Japanese school he had been accustomed to saying "*Sensei onegaishimasu*" (Please teach me) at the beginning of each lesson, and "*Arigatoo gozaimasu*" (Thank you for the lesson) at the end, he always said "Thank you" to the Australian teacher as he left the classroom. As a teacher myself, I can appreciate the reaction of the Australian teachers to this!

A constant source of amazement to me in our experience with the Japanese primary school was how quickly children learn to operate with a new set of values. When Andy and I were first alone in Tokyo, I was trying to live within a budget and would often run out of money before the end of the week. Andy had a piggy bank from which I would borrow on those occasions, and this made him extremely cross. I enjoyed the priorities—not to mention the rates themselves—in the following table of interest rates he proposed to charge me if I continued to borrow money from him:

Time	Education	Food	Other
1 day–7 days	15%	25%	35%
1–2 weeks	20%	30%	40%
2–3 weeks	25%	35%	45%
Over 3 weeks	30%	40%	50%

All in all, the experience was a wonderful one for Andy and for me. This is not to say that similar experiences would necessarily be the norm. It must be pointed out that the area in which we lived was a wealthy area in the center of Tokyo, and the school had a progressive principal and open-minded parents and teachers. I have heard that experiences vary considerably according to the area in Japan and (as anywhere in the world) the people encountered. One would have to acknowledge, too, that the experience for Andy was very different from that of the Japanese children: he had all the benefits of the Japanese primary school without the concurrent stress caused by the exam-oriented system experienced by some of his peers.

Looking back on the experience six months after he left Japan, Andy's independent reflections were as follows:

> It was a good experience, I thought, and a valuable one, as it really altered my life and the way in which I act. What was interesting was the actual schooling part of my experi-

ence. Whilst I was studying, I was fretting that I would be behind in my studies when I got back to Australia, for at that time some dumb kids in our class were holding us back, and we were behind in work we were supposed to do. But when I got to Australia, I found that I was actually ahead, and realized that it wasn't the actual work that makes the Japanese system succeed, but the way in which they prepare you in study/learning habits. Another thing I found on returning to Australia was that Australians were in a way more casual than the Japanese. They dared "rag" the teachers, or speak badly of them. They were more strict in Australia as far as punishments were concerned. In Australia they would give people Friday [one-hour] or Saturday [two- to three-hour] detentions, whichever most suited the "crime" the student had committed. In Japan, though, they had taught us not to get into trouble in the first place,

Sixth-grade farewell photo.

and we used to talk things over with our class instead of receive detentions.

When I think about my experience in the Japanese school, I think of a relaxed place where I mostly felt welcome and part of the community. Overall, I think it was a very valuable experience for me, and I very much appreciate what the teachers in Japan taught me.

THE PRIMARY SCHOOL EXPERIENCE FOR JAPANESE CHILDREN

Japanese society was one of the most powerful, intricate, and intense we had ever experienced. It appeared to be like a set of interlocking links to a chain. As such, it required that each child be taught to function in each link to be a part of the chain. The most fundamental link appeared to be the Japanese primary school, where the values of the society were firmly implanted to stand the child in good stead for the passage through the successive links of junior high school, high school, and university, then on to an eventual position in the corporation or as one of society's caregivers.

For the Japanese child, the primary school offered a basic preparation in both knowledge and socializing, particularly emphasizing the essentials for functioning in the Japanese group. It provided a nurturing environment which allowed time for each child to develop motivation for inquiry and learning, while at the same time developing group-interaction skills. The primary school created a bonding in its family environment and its role as the nucleus of the wider community, and at the same time offered a rich and caring center for learning in which there was little competition, thus allowing children to flourish in the ideal way educators would wish.

However, in considering the primary-school experience for Japanese children, we must consider their experience in all its perspectives, and that of course includes the part played by the cram school (*juku*) system. For those children for whom the objective was tertiary education, it seemed that the primary school alone was not considered adequate as preparation for later commitments in Japanese society. That is to say, the primary school had become too weak as a link in the chain. Its dual mission of adequate preparation in both socializing skills and knowledge was not being fulfilled, as the entrance exams for both high school and university had become increasingly difficult and demanding in terms of factual knowledge. Thus the cram school system was introduced, and with its advent came the competition which was lacking in the primary school itself, along with the rigid and stressful life that idealists abhor.

The experience for each Japanese child varied according to when and if the parents decided on entering the child into the *juku* system. While we were in Japan, some parents had their children streamed into that system as early as kindergarten. I heard that, in consequence, the teachers of the streamed kindergartners were paid higher salaries than other kindergarten and primary school teachers, because both teaching and "nursing" skills were required! Most of these very early streaming procedures were attached to private schools, ultimately feeding the hierarchically placed universities. One of these private schools was located near the university where I was teaching. I observed, with some pity, small children aged three to five years on my bus each morning, memorizing stories and numbers on the way to school, assisted by their mothers. Most of the children who entered cram school began around third or fourth grade of primary school. Some began as late as junior high school. From the time they entered this competitive environment, it appeared to me that the primary school experience for the Japanese children became very stressful; a long way from the rosy picture painted by many academic researchers and others interested in Japanese society.

Take, for example, an article from *The Japan Times* of 8 May 1993, entitled "Elementary-level Education Here Is Ideal: U.S. Scholar," in which Joy M. Tadaki reported on the findings of a prominent research psychologist and adjunct associate professor at the University of California, San Francisco, Dr. Catherine Lewis. Tadaki reported:

> While the stereotypical image of Japanese education recalls bespectacled students, cramming to join the prestigious university elite, Lewis says her research into how Japanese children become self-disciplined has proved that youngsters are not initially bound by such restrictions.

In our experience, it is the concept "initially" which is the variable factor, since although the restrictions were not imposed in the primary school itself, they were certainly imposed whenever the parents made the decision to enroll their children in the cram school; from that moment, the stereotype of the bespectacled student certainly began to become a reality.

Dr. Lewis has been responsible for some invaluable research into the Japanese primary school system, and I am one of her greatest admirers. At the inaugural Tane Matsu-kata Memorial Lecture given by her on April 9, 1993, at the Nishimachi International School in Tokyo, she com-pared the way mathematics was taught in Japan and the United States, as follows:

> Studies of Japanese elementary mathematics instruc-tion reveal that teachers cover only one or a few problems during a typical class, but allow children to raise and debate their own ideas, and to derive mathematical ideas themselves.... This differs sharply from practice in many American classrooms, where the teacher gives the formula and students do many practice problems—but where mathematics achieve-ment is ultimately much lower.

I wonder whether the Japanese achievement would be as high without the cram school system. As I explained ear-lier, Andy was attending one of the least stressful cram school systems for both mathematics and Japanese lan-guage, and was ahead of what was being taught in the Japanese primary school class because of this. The top stu-dents in his class were all attending the more competitive cram schools. Perhaps, then, we might have to consider that it was a combination of the primary school and the cram school which produced such high results in mathe-matics for the Japanese.

Other researchers, while not focusing particularly on the primary school, have expressed what I feel are some-what distorted views about Japanese education. The Aus-tralian professor, Robert March, in his book *Working for a Japanese Company* (Kodansha International, 1992) talks about Japanese education as follows:

> The focus of Japanese education is on factual reten-
> tion. Issues are not discussed. The focus of the
> school room is on the children being good boys and
> girls, behaving properly, pleasing teacher, being on
> good terms with one another and certainly not fight-
> ing. (p. 199)

Our experience was different both with regard to exclusive
focus on factual retention and with regard to behavior. In
the primary school itself, the focus was a balance of academic preparation and socializing skills gained through the
learning process. Because the entrance exam demanded
factual retention, it constrained the parents to supplement
the factual knowledge learned by the children in the
school with extra preparation from the cram schools. However, in the classroom issues were discussed at length—
the learning process was of prime importance. The picture
of harmony in the classroom painted by March was not
our experience with the Japanese primary school. Indeed,
from an outside observer's point of view, the Japanese
classroom might sometimes have appeared a wild and unruly environment. We learned that this was merely a way
of allowing the children to come to terms with their own
guidelines to behavioral norms in Japanese society. Perhaps, then, the stereotypical image described by March
was more attributable to the middle-school and/or high-
school links in the Japanese societal chain than to the
Japanese primary school.

At this point it might be useful to consider the cost of
implementing the dual system of primary school and
cram school involved for the Japanese child. Here, I would
offer two considerations, stress and loss of childhood. The

pressures of the cram school appeared to affect the students' attitudes to learning and their health. Children seemed to love the actual subject matter being studied in the cram school, but resented the fact that it had to be learned to pass an entrance exam. As a result, motivation to learning was exam-oriented and learning itself was associated with tension and stress. Furthermore, those children with heavy cram-school commitments were so tired that they were often reluctant participants in the primary school classroom. They also seemed to resent their lack of free time to play and be children, and I often wondered whether this might have been a reason for what appeared to be childish behavior later in life, both at university and in work environments.

Some Thoughts on the Future of Primary Education in Japan

Change, along with time, is inevitable. However, I am not a believer in change for change's sake, and I feel that we are currently in an age of such rapid change and fast communication that we sometimes ignore the value of wisdom acquired over time in favor of revolutionary change, and tend to throw out the baby with the bath water. In my view, improvements are made through innovation resting on a strong foundation of experience. Any changes to the Japanese primary school must therefore first recognize its inherent qualities. Furthermore, because the Japanese primary school is only the first link in the chain that forms the education system, any change in the primary school must inevitably involve changes in each of the successive links of junior high, high school, university, and corporation. Accordingly, I would like to review what I see as the current status of Japanese primary school within the education system, suggest why there might be need for change in it and the whole system, outline some possible changes in each link, and reflect on some implications of such changes for the society.

The Current Status of the Primary School

A history of isolation meant that the Japanese were able to concentrate on perfecting an education system to suit the needs of their own society, a system that focused on helping one's own and ignoring the needs of outsiders. The system depended on a longer school year, a national curriculum, respect for teachers as educators, and family support for education. The restructuring of the economy after World War II has been built around the needs of corporations and the state, with the consequence that education has come to be driven increasingly by their demands. The *kaisha* (corporation) offers its own training program for all new employees recruited from the hierarchically ranked universities and depends on pre-university education for the basic preparation of its employees. In the postwar education system, there are five basic links to the chain forming this system, of which the primary school is the first and possibly most crucial. Initially, the primary school provided socializing skills along with basic knowledge which was later developed through junior high and high school toward passing the university entrance exam. The university itself gradually came to be viewed as a playground, more important for the name of the university and its place in the university hierarchy—which eventually determined the quality of one's job—than for the tertiary education it provided. In later years, the university entrance exam became increasingly more difficult, necessitating the introduction of the cram-school system from primary school to supplement factual knowledge.

The system as a whole is much admired by many prominent scholars and organizations as one that produces the highest literacy rate in the world and has led to the development of an extraordinarily powerful economy in a relatively short time. In late 1993, the United Nations ranked Japan as one of the top countries in child education. At that time, former prime minister Toshiki Kaifu said that it had been Japan's policy of promoting education which had been the foundation of its development. Sadako Ogata, the U.N. high commissioner for refugees and former dean of the Faculty of Foreign Studies and Professor of International Relations at Tokyo's Sophia University, reflecting on Japanese primary and secondary education, says:

> The strength of primary and secondary education in Japan lies in the thoroughness with which basic knowledge is inculcated in a wide range of students[12]

It would seem, then, that with such an ideal system there would be no need for change. However, there are many in Japanese society who advocate change, and for good reasons.

The Need for Change

Although up until recently the education system has adequately served the needs of its users, developments in two major areas would seem to indicate a need for some change.

First, the Japanese government has recognized a need for internationalization; there is now constant contact with outsiders, whereas the education system was set up in a period of relative isolation from the rest of the world. Second, the personal needs of Japanese students themselves have also changed.

In an era of high technology and economic success, Japan is also trying to make its place in the international political arena. Japanese corporations, the needs of which seem to have determined the current status of the education system, are increasingly moving toward globalization, particularly as the yen has become stronger. In consequence, there is need for a work force made up of people who are educated to communicate internationally and who are open to operating in the international community. Creative, deductive thinkers are required to assume responsibility in a more flexible environment. The national curriculum has so far been able to prepare Japanese students thoroughly for a somewhat narrow environment in which values were fairly homogeneous. There has been little tolerance of difference within the Japanese group and little or no preparation in how to deal with difference outside it other than through objectives of homogeneity. As we move toward the challenges of the twenty-first century, young people are required to compete in a global arena with other young people from all over the world, demanding flexibility and competent skills in intercultural interaction.

Most educators and parents worldwide are concerned about preparation of students to be global citizens of tomorrow, and here I would like to reflect on some comments of two prominent educators. At the Inaugural Tane

Matsukata Memorial Lecture in Tokyo, on April 9, 1993, Dr. Catherine Lewis of the University of California introduced her talk with a most interesting rhetorical question and observation focusing on objectives for education:

> Think of the children you know who are now in their elementary and middle school years. What qualities would you like them to have fifteen or twenty years from now? I am impressed that diverse parents, from many different ethnic groups, wealthy and poor, urban and rural, share very similar aspirations for their children. They want them to be principled and responsible. They want them to be kind and caring. They want them to have great knowledge about the world, and to have self-discipline, skill, and motivation to keep learning throughout life.

In a lecture entitled "Education for What?" organized again by the Nishimachi International School in November 1993, Dr. Eric Anderson, Headmaster of Eton College in Windsor, England, listed guidelines he considered important in education:

1. We must not neglect factual learning.
2. Facts by themselves are no longer enough; there are four additional objectives:
   a) solving problems;
   b) how to learn;
   c) how to think for oneself;
   d) how to think again about what was thought before.
3. School is not the end, it's the beginning. Students should be motivated to go on learning.

4. Education does not begin and end with rational learning. Besides rational intelligence there is musical, practical, interpersonal, athletic, and other kinds of intelligence.
5. Modern education has to be both national and international; education begins at home first.
6. We must not neglect moral education.
7. Schools have a duty to provide a "habitual vision of greatness"—that is to say, to present the best role models to counteract the many negative role models students get in society such as images of cruelty, selfishness, and triviality.

These comments advocate the need for qualities of good citizenship, a broad knowledge base, and motivation to continue learning. In short, educators around the globe are very concerned with preparing students to take their places in the international community and are very aware of the range of skills and the versatility with which each student needs to be equipped.

Policies of internalization also imply successful intercultural communication skills. In general, the Japanese do not interact well with foreigners. When communicating in English, this is not due to lack of preparation in knowledge of grammar or vocabulary but rather to a lack of experience in interpersonal communication with foreigners and to an original communication style founded in a rather unique, and certainly very rigid, set of choices. The responsibility for this inability to communicate in foreign languages lies also with the objectives of the language program itself and with the perception of foreigners as outsiders. There is no introduction to the joys of communicating in a foreign language even in middle school, much less in primary school. Rather, a language is ultimately viewed in the same way as any other academic subject, as something which has to be learned to pass an exam. The attitude to the foreigner is still basically one of exclusion, which results among other things in an unfortunate tendency on the part of the Japanese, when communicating with foreigners, to want to be given knowledge and helped through communication without reciprocating.

If the ultimate objectives of the education system are determined by the needs of the *kaisha*, and these needs are to be nested in globalization, then this will also be reflected in the need for changes in all links of the system. The university must inevitably become more internationally competitive; the secondary schools need to take a broader, less exam-focused orientation; and the primary school will need to maintain its original balance between knowledge acquisition and socializing skills, while introducing students to a broader world vision.

One of the prime concerns in the need for change should be Japanese children themselves. In November 1995, a marked increase in suicides among young people, particularly in the fourteen to nineteen age bracket, was reported. The most common reason given was performance in school, followed by worries over entrance examinations and troubles in relationships with friends. Even in primary school, the stress the children could suffer was exacerbated by a contradiction between what they could afford (economic power) and what was unavailable to them in terms of recreation and leisure activities. There is certainly a need for greater balance between academic achievements and leisure pursuits, and I wonder if children need to have their focus directed so early towards their adult life. It seems a pity that the objective of a primary school child can already be his or her ultimate position in adult society, and involve directing all time and energy toward passing a university entrance exam which effectively determines the ultimate possibilities for the individual in society.

What Kinds of Changes are Required?

Again, the most useful starting point here is the work environment, preparation for which is the ultimate goal of the system. It would seem that a purely Japanese management system will not satisfy the future needs of companies in an era of globalization. While the merits of the Japanese corporation's organizational principles are well recognized, there are indications that some sort of hybrid system based on a combination of Japanese and Western principles will probably emerge. If so, the corporation will no longer look only at the name of the university from which its prospective employee emerges, but increasingly at the preparation of the individual himself. In other words, universities will increasingly function less as recreational facilities and more as institutions of higher learning with emphasis on quality research, study skills, and creativity. Competition for places in the corporation will move from the university entrance exam to the job market. Without the "rest" which is currently available to students at university level, a more balanced curriculum at junior-high and high-school levels will be required to reduce stress and unpleasant associated phenomena such as bullying. It is also likely that in reducing overall stress, some provision will be made for streaming gifted students and students of special talents in areas outside academia.

At the primary-school level, these changes will necessitate the introduction of a curriculum with a broader and more international knowledge base, early introduction of foreign languages, and a more flexible socializing environment.

In discussions concerning change, some Japanese have advocated a move toward the *juku*-type school and the abolishment of the primary-school system as it stands now, arguing that the material learned in the *juku* is much more interesting to the children than what is learned in the primary school. Their argument thus focuses entirely on curriculum rather than on socializing skills. It is apparent that the *juku* system emerged as a result of the ever-increasing competition for places in the hierarchically ranked educational institutions. However, the *juku* system is exactly what it purports to be—a cram-school system—and as such could never substitute for the primary school, where the rigid socializing values required to operate in Japanese society are imparted, even if the society were to become more flexible. A move toward a more exam-oriented primary school, by abolishing the *juku* system and making the primary school an imitation of it, would therefore no longer prepare the children socially and would only serve to increase stress. University and training in the corporation involve a reinforcement of the initial socializing and practical skills learned in primary school but increasingly neglected later in favor of exam-directed learning, indicating that in Japanese adult society these socializing skills are extremely important. At the same time, abolishing the *juku* system altogether and retaining the socializing focus would mean redefining the university entrance exam, with the consequent restructuring of university education and the progression from university to the world of employment.

Implications for Change

The implications of the sort of changes mentioned above will be different at each link in the chain.

At the level of the corporation, there will be more competition for places based on skills, and training systems within the organization will be adjusted accordingly. The employee will be less rigidly committed to one organization, and there will be facility of movement for employees from one organization to another within Japan as well as internationally.

Changes in the universities will produce students who are more internationally competitive and more balanced in their preparation. An emphasis on creativity and job competition might also lead students to more specialized preparation, facilitating international study at all levels of tertiary education.

In the junior high schools and high schools there should be a place for everybody according to his/her talents, and in consequence less bullying with more acceptance of difference.

In the primary schools, if gifted students are allowed to advance and the university entrance exam is no longer the ultimate objective of studies, then there should be no need for the cram-school system, thus allowing the focus to rest on the balance of knowledge and socializing skills which we found to be so attractive.

Changes are reflected in various ways in societies. Already, as a result of international contact, a gradual change is taking place with regard to the heretofore distinctly defined roles in Japanese society. Although education will, I am sure, always be a high priority in Japan, family support in terms of the physical presence of the mothers has already begun to dwindle; because the dedication of mothers to their children's education is one of the strongest supports to the society in preparing the next generation to enter the work force, this change in roles is already having an impact on the system. Women are not as prepared to give up career prospects for educating children, nor are they as prepared even to get married and have children in a system which relegates them to this task so rigidly. The role of the teacher and the student-teacher relationship are also being questioned. When students begin to be encouraged to speak out and give opinions independently, the role of the teacher as possessor of absolute wisdom is in jeopardy, although this does not yet seem to have eroded the professionalism of educators in the primary schools.

Change in a system also demands change in associated societal values. The Japanese have always set very high standards for themselves, and are renowned for aspiring to perfection. There comes a certain point, however, when the human being reaches the limit of what is possible, and it seems to me that the Japanese system is stretching its participants to the maximum. Therefore, any additional input to the curriculum must result in giving up something already in place. The high standards of learning in the Japanese language might need to be reduced to allow time, for example, to introduce more effective foreign-language learning to the curriculum. This will be difficult, as we have already witnessed with the introduction of the second and fourth Saturdays of the month as vacations in the move toward a five-day school week; the Saturday hours were simply added into the Monday-to-Friday program to compensate. However, some relaxation of standards (and therefore of pressure on students) may be required to satisfy the needs of students in a global village where they might like to enjoy intercultural communication both in face-to-face situations and in situations provided by technology, such as the Internet.

Changes will inevitably occur, but these will be slow and measured, and, we hope, will not destroy what we found to be an excellent primary school system. No education system is ever perfect, and all are constantly under scrutiny. Theoretically, the ideal system would be one in which the needs of each child were catered to individually. Since this is impossible in practical terms, parents and teachers must act sensitively in making choices for children in any system. Among the choices available, the Japanese system, at the primary-school level, is certainly one of the better.

EPILOGUE

Andy left Japan at the end of January 1994 to enter a school in Brisbane, Australia. Both the Japanese friends he had left behind and others who had been interested in his experience wondered how Andy would readjust to the Australian education system and to socializing with his peers in Australia. Therefore, I think it appropriate here to describe in some detail his new educational environment.

His new school is a private boys' school within the Brisbane diocese of the Anglican church. It is also a boarding school with approximately 350 of its 1,400 students being boarders. Since I remained in Japan in my teaching position, Andy joined the school as a boarder. Most of the boarders are from areas outside the Brisbane city area, within the state of Queensland, but others also come from overseas, particularly Taiwan, Papua New Guinea, and Indonesia. There are also several Japanese boys boarding and some other Japanese students as day boys. The new experience thus involved an adjustment not only to the education system but also to the new lifestyle in a new community.

Andy embraced his new situation with enthusiasm, and his reentry was facilitated by the kindness of the educators and by the fact that all those beginning in the first year of junior high school were making similar adjustments. Parents of new boarders are invited to sleep over at the school with the boys the weekend before school begins to participate in an orientation program. This later allows parents to share the context of the school environment with their sons more readily through letters and telephone calls.

Naturally, supervision of boarding-school students demands a fairly rigid set of rules for the junior boarders, but Andy did not find this a problem after the strict infrastructure of the Japanese system. Boys have set meal times, and generally speaking the food is good. There is a general daily routine throughout the week, sports on Saturdays, and day excursions on Sundays. Boys have limited pocket money and exit permissions.

Socializing among his peers was perhaps not as difficult as it had been in Japan, but nevertheless required some adjusting to required behavioral patterns. Whereas in Japan, people were immediately categorized as different and treated accordingly, in Australia difference seemed to be minimized but in an equally ethnocentric way. Thus it seemed to be expected that boys joining the school from outside Australia, with no experience in operating in the Australian school system, much less a boarding-school environment, would make the adjustment with little or no assistance. Andy's Japanese experience and his behavioral manifestations of it led to his being initially called "the Japanese" by more senior students and to his often siding with the Asian students. One issue arose over the type of rice the boys were being offered in the dining room. The Asian group including Andy complained to the boarding master that the rice was not of sufficiently good quality, resulting in the Asian group being given a special allotment of quality rice. Interestingly, shortly afterwards, the other boys realized that there was a difference and asked for the same privilege.

The very rigid *senpai-kōhai* system operating in Japanese society is often described as unique, but in Australian boys' boarding schools a similar system is in operation, based on the British tradition. The senior boys in Australian schools not only take on a leadership role but, in doing so, often administer physical and mental challenges in exercising their newfound authority. The Australian school tends to play this behavior down, while being in tacit agreement with its operation, whereas the Japanese one makes an open commitment to its value. In any case, Andy's training with the *senpai-kōhai* system stood him in great stead for dealing with his position on the lowest rung of the ladder in the Australian school. On occasion the seniors in the dormitories would "borrow" the younger boys' radios and cassette players, make offensive remarks about them, or give them the odd punch in the arm and other such mild physical actions in exerting their authority. As in Japan, the senior sometimes abuses his position more severely.

There are considerable advantages to living on the school grounds: one can participate in more of the extracurricular activities offered in sports, music, chess, debating, public speaking, speech and drama, and others. Sports are organized around three sporting seasons. In the first, when it is still hot, they offer swimming, rowing, cricket, and volleyball. In the cooler second season they offer rugby, Australian rules football, soccer, and cross-country running, and in the third (spring) the sports are basketball, tennis, and water polo. Andy takes swimming, soccer, and basketball. In addition, boarders can use the sporting facilities in their spare time when available.

The music program at his new school is excellent. Andy

has been able to continue his violin lessons with a wonderful teacher. He is also enjoying membership in the school orchestra, a senior string group, and a smaller chamber music group. The choir is also good, and there are several less-formal singing groups and numerous other possibilities for participation in activities of the music department.

In the school system in the state of Queensland, high school is not divided into junior high and high school: there are rather five years of high school with an important examination at the end of year 10 and another at the end of year 12. Places at university are allotted according to the results of these exams. Tertiary institutions and departments can require varying entrance scores. At Andy's school, the formal academic program had been designed to meet some of the aims of the school and placed particular emphasis on the needs of students. Needs identified in the school curriculum booklet were:

1. The need to be able to communicate in both words and symbols: English (including computing), modern languages, and mathematics (including computing).
2. The need to be able to interact and understand the social and physical environment: social science (including both history and geography), science.
3. The need to understand the meaning of life: religious education.
4. The need to have a healthy mind and body: health, fitness, game skills.
5. The need to explore individual talents and interests in (a) the fine arts: art, music, film and video, speech and drama; (b) the practical arts: graphics, woodwork, metalwork, carpentry; (c) other areas:

business principles and practice, agricultural science, computer applications.

Based on these needs, in years 8, 9, and 10 all boys take a "core" course of the following:

English   Science
Mathematics   Religious education
A modern language   Health, fitness, game skills
Social science

In addition, all students in year 8 are given an introduction to the secondary courses in art, drama, music, graphics, woodwork, and metalwork. In years 9 and 10, the "core" course continues and a choice is made of one of the following electives. The same elective may be studied for both years, or a different one chosen each year.

Agricultural science   Music
Art   Woodwork
Business principles   Metalwork
Film and video   Speech and drama
Graphics

In general, promotion from year 8 to 9 and from 9 to 10 is automatic, except for exceptional circumstances such as protracted illness or complete inability to cope with work. However, promotion from year 10 to 11 and from 11 to 12 requires a minimum achievement score.

In years 11 and 12, students study six subjects, one selected from each of the six columns below. All students in year 11 take religious education and two one-semester elective subjects.

1	2	3	4	5	6
English	Maths I	Maths II	Physics	Accounting	Accounting
	Maths A	Modern history	Economics	Chemisty	Art
		Biological science	Multi-strand science	Geography	Biological science
		Agriculture	Graphics	Health & physical ed.	French
		Film and TV	Chemistry	Physics	German
		Practical computer methods	Ancient history	Legal studies	Indonesian
		Earth science	Drama	Information processing & technology	Japanese
		Music	Australian studies	Business studies	Geography
			Geography	Study of religion	Modern history
					Technology studies
					Engineering

With regard to modern languages, the curriculum booklet states:

> It is the policy of the school for students to study a modern language, at least to the end of Year 9, and in general to the end of Year 10. Only in exceptional cases, where a student's performance in a modern language and in the core subjects is very poor, will a student ... be allowed to change this pattern of course selection.

Boys at the school come from numerous primary schools, all of which have different policies with regard to the learning of modern language languages. Some boys already have a good grounding in a language, while others are learning a language for the first time. A choice of four compulsory languages—Indonesian, Japanese, French, and German—is offered and, since each is for beginners, Andy chose to study Bahasa Indonesian in class and Japanese by correspondence from outside, through Kumon. Languages are studied under continuous assessment in the state of Queensland, and when Andy started there we found that he could not be credited with his Japanese unless he attended the beginners class, since only students who had been continuously assessed throughout a year by teachers could gain credit for the language. Under the government policies of encouraging young Australians to know as many languages as possible, this system seemed to me to be both counterproductive and a disincentive to those students who already had some degree of proficiency in a language. The teachers certainly did not want them in the beginners classes and more advanced classes were not being offered, so there was no acknowledgement of their mastery of the language. I raised the question with the school and, after some negotiation between the school and the Secondary Schools' Board, it was decided that students could be credited with the language on their school reports by taking the exams outside class time. Thus, on language-exam day, Andy takes the Japanese test before school and the Bahasa Indonesian test during class.

Academically, he did not seem to be behind the other boys, even in subjects such as social studies and English, where I had expected some problems in expression and spelling as well as lack of preparation in content areas. The science curriculum is different from the Japanese one but equally interesting and, Andy felt, on a similar level. However, in math he found he had covered what was being offered, and asked to be re-enrolled in the Brisbane Kumon (Japanese cram school) for some extra math for the first six months. After that he found that he had enough to do in balancing everything going on around him, and decided to stop and just concentrate on class studies. As he moved into year 9, he found that he was no longer advantaged in having done some of the work; with a considerable amount of regular homework required, he found the curriculum challenging. He chose business principles for his elective and is enjoying it very much.

In the private-school system in Queensland there are four school holiday periods each year: two weeks in March/April for Easter, three weeks from mid-June to early July, two weeks in September/October, and a long summer holiday from early December until early February. Andy continues to return to Japan twice each year, during the June and December school holidays, for three weeks each time, to study in the Japanese junior high school where many of his friends from primary school attend. Once again, we were very lucky to find a principal at the junior high school who was willing to allow him this privilege, and Andy very much enjoys the opportunity to use his Japanese language, meet up again with his friends, and interact in Japanese society.

APPENDIX

Who Is Eligible to Attend Japanese Primary School?

Anybody living in Japan and holding an alien registration card is entitled to send their children to Japanese primary school in the ward shown in the address on the card. Except in special cases, each child should attend the school closest to the family residence. However, under the regulations, a child may not be enrolled in more than one school at the same time. If a parent would like the child to attend Japanese school as a guest on Saturdays, during the school holidays, or at any other time, the possibility of doing so seems to depend on the principal of the school in question. Some Japanese schools are very interested in attracting foreign students in the move toward internationalization in Japan, but others feel that foreigners present too many problems, especially where learning the Japanese language is concerned. I was told that it is easier with native English speakers than with speakers of other languages, where the teacher fears that he/she will not be able to communicate with the child.

The authorities at our ward office have stressed, on many occasions, the importance of timing in the Japanese curriculum. That is to say, foreigners must not hold up the class so that the Japanese students do not cover the study required within the time limits stipulated by the Ministry of Education. One cannot expect great amounts of extra time to be dedicated to the foreigner who does not understand the language.

How Do I Get In?

If full-time education in the Japanese primary school is required, one must go to the ward (local government) office education department, and fill out an application form. An example of the form used in our ward appears on page 218, with instructions on how to fill it out in example 1. The form may vary from ward to ward, but the information required will be basically the same. The office will notify the school, and the child appears on the appropriate day at the school with the completed form in hand.

Example 1
(1) Date of application (year / month / day).
(2) Name of next of kin.
(3) Signature of next of kin.
(4) Address of next of kin.
(5) Telephone number of next of kin.
(6) Name of child (in *kana* for the Japanese).
(7) At 7, there are two pairs of *kanji* and you must circle one pair. The left pair refers to primary student; the right pair means junior-high student (for Australians, the first three years of high school).
(8) Name of child (in *kanji* for the Japanese, in the Roman alphabet if foreign).
(9) Date of birth (year / month / day).
(10) Japanese name. Some foreign students, typically Chinese and Korean, have been asked to take a Japanese name. Other foreigners would leave this blank.

係　員	学事係長	庶務係長	学務課長	庶務課長	次　長

外 国 人 就 学 願

① 平成　　年　　月　　日

東京都港区教育委員会　殿

② 保護者氏名 ＿＿＿＿＿＿＿＿＿＿＿＿　③印

④ 住　　　所 ＿＿＿＿＿＿＿＿＿＿＿＿

⑤ 電話（　　　）＿＿＿＿＿＿＿＿

下記のとおり就学させたいのでお願いいたします。

記

⑥ フリガナ		生年月日	⑨ 昭和　　年　　月　　日
⑦児童・生徒 ⑧氏　　名			
⑩通 称 名		性　別	⑪男・女
⑫国　　籍		外国人登録番号	⑬
⑭住　　所			
入学希望校及び学年	⑮港区立　　小・中	⑯　　学校　第⑰学年	
在学校名	平成 ⑱ 年　月　日 ⑲　　⑳ 学校　第 ㉑ 学年 ㉒ 在学/修了		
保護者名	㉓	続柄 ㉔	㉕ 男/女

上記の者、本校第　　学年に就学することに支障ありません。

　　　　東京都港区立　　　　　　　　学校長　　　　印

東京都港区教育委員会　殿

学校所見		処理月日	受理	・
			許可	・
			通知	・

(11) Gender. The left *kanji* means male, and the right, female.

(12) Nationality.

(13) Alien registration card number.

(14) Home address of student.

(15) Name of school you wish to enter.

(16) Whether primary or junior high. The top *kanji* means primary and the bottom junior high.

(17) Grade you wish to enter. (Sometimes the Japanese authorities will advise you to put your child in a grade lower than his current grade because of language difficulties.)

(18) Date of transfer.

(19) Name of last school.

(20) Whether last school was primary or junior high.

(21) Grade at last school.

(22) There are two pairs of kanji. Circle the top pair if the child left without finishing the grade. Circle the bottom pair if the child finished the grade.

(23) Name of next of kin.

(24) Relationship of child to next of kin.

(25) Gender. Circle the top *kanji* if male, and the bottom if female.

At the school, you are required to fill out a second form (pp. 220–22). The one we filled out is shown with explanations below.

Example 2
Page 1
The circle in the top left-hand corner means that the in-

秘

児 童 調 査 票

港区立本村小学校
学年　　組
No.（　　　）

平成　　年　　月調査

| 児童 | ① 氏名 ふりがな | | ② 男・女 | ③ 昭和　年　月　日生 |
| | ④ 現住所 | 区　　　町　丁目　　番　号 | | |

保護者	⑤ 氏名 ふりがな		電話 ⑥	
	⑦ 職業		児童からみた続柄 ⑧	
	⑨ 現住所	（児童とちがう場合のみ）		

⑩ 入学前の経歴 ⑪	(a)　年　月より		
	(b)　年　月まで	(c) 幼稚園在園	
	年　月より		
	年　月まで	保育園在園	

家族（本人を除いてください）	氏　　　名	児童との関係	年令	職業または在学校名（本校在学者は学年・組をかく）
		⑫ 父	⑬	⑭
		母		

学校までの略図（通学所要時間　　分）通学路を赤書き ⑮	緊急な場合の連絡方法（TEL）
	⑯ 自宅　（　）
	⑰ 呼出　（　）　　　　様
	⑱ 勤務先など　（　）
	欠席の場合、連絡する友だち
	⑲　年　組（　　　） 　年　組（　　　）

formation may not be disclosed to anyone other than the teachers.

(1) Name of the child in syllabic script (*katakana*), if possible.

(2) Gender. Circle the top *kanji* if male and the bottom if female.

(3) Date of birth (year / month/ day).

(4) Home address.

(5) Name of next of kin.

(6) Telephone number of next of kin.

(7) Occupation of next of kin.

(8) Relationship of next of kin to student.

(9) Address of next of kin, where different from that of the child.

(10) Previous schools attended and dates. There are places for the two most recent schools. At (a) write the year and month of commencement. At (b) write the year and month of completion. At (c) write the name of the school and the place (e.g., The British School, Indonesia).

(11) Family member's name.

(12) Relationship to child.

(13) Age.

(14) Occupation. If still studying, in what institution, in which grade, in which section (e.g., primary, 3rd grade, 2nd section).

(15) Map showing how to get to your address from the school. Emergency telephone numbers.

(16) Home telephone number.

(17) Extension number (especially for those families in company housing).

(18) Office telephone number.

| 児童氏名 | | あてはまるところを○でかこんでください。
空らんはあてはまることを書いてください。 |

健康のようす	① 健　　康	健康でじょうぶ　　　　ふつう　　弱い	
	② 睡　　眠	ねる時刻　　　　時　　　おきる時刻　③　　　時	
	④ 偏　　食	ない　少しある　多い　偏食するもの　⑤	
	⑥ 今までかかった 　主な病気	はしか（　才）　百日咳（　才）　水痘（　才） 消化不良　　自家中毒　　ひきつけ　　風疹 その他（　）	
	⑦ 現在かかって いる病気など	ない　　ある　　ある 　　　　　　　　場合	
	⑧ 健康について注 意してほしい点		
家庭生活のようす	⑨ 友　だ　ち	だれとでもよく遊ぶ　一人で遊ぶ　　すきな 　　　　　　　　　　　　　　　　　　遊び　⑩	
	⑪ 仲よしの友だち		
	⑫ 興味・趣味	絵をかく　本を読む　うたをうたう　ものを作る　その他	
	⑬ こづかい	与えていない　与えている　　与え 　　　　　　　　　　　　　　　　かた　⑭	
	⑮ 家での手伝い	しない　　する　　どんな 　　　　　　　　　　手伝い　⑯	
	⑰ し　つ　け	きびしい　ふつう　　こどもまかせ	
	⑱ 家庭学習	ほとんどしない　いわれてする　自分からする（　時間位）	
	⑲ テ　レ　ビ	ほとんどみない　きめてみる　みてばかりいる（　時間位）	
	⑳ 学習塾・おけいこ	行っていない　行っている　　習っている 　　　　　　　　　　　　　　　　も　の　㉑	
性格・行動のようす	長所と思われ る点やよい習 慣など	㉒	
	短所と思われ る点やわるい 習慣など	㉓	
教育へのご意見など	現在いちばん 力を入れてい る点	㉔	
	教育について 学校に要望し たいこと・ご 意見など	㉕	
備考	㉖		

(19) Telephone numbers of two other children in the school who live nearby.

Page 2

(1) General condition of health. Circle one: healthy, normal, weak.

(2) What time does the child usually go to sleep?

(3) What time does the child usually wake up?

(4) Are there any special problems with food? (None, a few, plenty.)

(5) Are there any particular foods the child loves or hates?

(6) Circle any of the following from which the child might have suffered, and if possible write the child's age at the time.

Measles (   )   Whooping cough (   )
Chicken pox (   )
Indigestion (   )   Food poisoning (   )
Convulsions (   )   Rubella (   )
Other (   )

(7) a) Does he/she suffer from any illness at the moment? Circle the first two *hiragana* if the answer is no, and the second two if the answer is yes.

b) If the answer is yes, please explain.

(8) Does the child have any special requirements?

(9) Friends (plays with anyone, plays by himself).

(10) Something he especially likes playing.

(11) Name of his closest friend.

(12) What does he do in his spare time? (Draw, read, sing, make things, other.)

(13) Pocket money (receives, doesn't receive).

(14) How is pocket money given? (e.g., for helping, a regular amount, per week, per month, etc.)

(15) Does he help at home? (yes / no)

(16) What does he do to help?

(17) Discipline at home (strict, normal, relaxed).

(18) Study at home (not at all, under supervision, self motivated; how many hours).

(19) Television (never watches, watches what we choose, watches what he wants).

(20) Extra lessons (goes, does not go).

(21) What does he learn? (e.g., violin, singing).

Personality

(22) What are his good qualities?

(23) What are his bad qualities?

Expectations

(24) What do you consider to be the most important thing for the child in school life?

(25) What would you like the child to learn in school?

(26) Any other thoughts.

Recently, in some areas, the above information has been voted as an excessive invasion of privacy; in those areas, the following more simple form is required by the school:

Front

1) Name in syllabic script (*katakana*).

2) Name as it is usually written.

3) Home address.

4) Telephone number.

5) Grade.

6) Section.
7) Date of birth (year/month/day).
8) Gender (circle left *kanji* for male, right for female).
9) Name of next of kin and relationship.
10) Address.
11) If there are any brothers or sisters in the school give name and section in appropriate grade.
12) Previous school attended (from year/month to year/month).
13) Circle left *kanji* if private school, right *kanji* if public.
14) Circle left group of *kanji* if it was a kindergarten, right group if it was a nursery school.

No. _____

平成　　　　年度　　児童カード		⑤ 年　　⑥組	
児童	ふりがな ①	生　年　月　日	
	氏 名 ②	⑦ 昭・平　年 月 日	
		⑧ 性別：男　　女	
	現住所 ③ 〒（　　　）		
	電話 ④		
保護者	ふりがな		
	氏 名 ⑨		
	（続柄）		
	住所 ⑩ 〒（　　　）		

⑪本校在学中の兄弟・姉妹組・名前	1 年	2 年	3 年	4 年	5 年	6 年	若 竹	その他

入学前の経歴	平成 ⑫ 年　　月～　　年　　月まで
	私・公立 ⑬　　　　　　　　　⑭ 幼稚園・保育園（新1年生記入）

☆児童名簿、指導要録等の原票として使用しますので、楷書でお書き下さい。

家族構成（本人をのぞく）		通学路の略図
氏　名：学生は学年も	続柄	
⑮　　　　　⑯	⑰	
緊急な場合の連絡先		
順位	電　話　番　号	場　　所
1	⑱	⑲
2		
3		
4		
欠席の場合、連絡する方だち		
年　　組：氏名 ⑳		
年　　組：氏名	地域班	

Back

15) Family member's name.
16) If family member is a student, which grade.
17) Relationship of family member to student.
18) Telephone numbers to be used in emergency.
19) Place of emergency telephone number (home, office, other).
20) Grade, section, and name of two children attending the school who live nearby.

If part-time attendance is desired, the procedure is to make an appointment with the headmaster of the school and explain the reasons for your request in a sort of get-to-know-you meeting. If he feels comfortable with the situation, he will ask the Board of Education, and if they approve, you will be advised. If you are accepted, you will be required to fill out the forms described above, one for the ward office and one for the school.

Is English Spoken?

Yes. However, the Japanese sometimes need to be encouraged to communicate. All Japanese people have some knowledge of the English language, but even those who are actually very proficient often prefer not to use it. Writing and reading skills are generally much better than listening and speaking, so in attempting to communicate in English, it is often wise to write things down.

In some local government offices there are special sections and/or employees to deal with foreigners, and in these offices English, and often other languages, are spoken. In most offices, it would be wise to take an interpreter.

In the schools themselves, whether English is spoken or not will depend on the school and the staff. In primary schools, little or no language study is undertaken as yet and any English spoken will depend on the staff and on other parents and their children. Staff may be willing or unwilling to communicate in English. Often some families will have lived abroad, and these parents and children may be willing to communicate in English.

What Does It Cost?

It costs very little to attend Japanese primary school, as education is subsidized by the very high local income taxes, which are paid in addition to national tax.

Initial outlay is about ¥25,500 (A$335, US$255) for the following items (all prices in yen).

Summer hat		1,500
Winter hat		1,500
Swimming equipment		5,000
Swimming costume	1,500	
Swimming cap	500	
Goggles	1,500	
Swimming bag	500	
Swimming towel	1,000	
Sports equipment		6,500
Sports bag	500	
T-shirt	2,000	
Shorts	2,000	
Sports cap	500	
Sports shoes	1,500	
Keyboard		5,000
Recorder		2,000
Shūji (calligraphy) set		2,000
Sewing kit		2,000

The Japanese children do use a special school bag, modeled after the German/Swiss ranzel (in Japanese, *randoseru*), which is supposed to be the most expensive in the world at ¥30,000 (A$395, US$300). Although it is customary for the Japanese children to have one, I never bought one and had Andy use his Australian school bag, which never incited comments from anyone.

A monthly fee is payable to cover educational items such as notebooks, paints, and the daily hot lunch. The education part of it was fixed in our primary school at ¥800 (A$10, US$8); the hot lunch part varied slightly according to grade—grades 1 and 2 paid ¥3,180 (A$42, US$32), grades 3 and 4 paid ¥3,490 (A$46, US$35), and grades 5 and 6 paid ¥3,800 (A$50, US$38). Thus, for Andy's sixth grade, I was paying ¥4,600 (about A$61, US $46). In addition, on occasion (perhaps twice a year), one is asked to pay small sums of anything up to ¥1,000 (A$13, US$10) for excursions, and there is a fee for camp in grades 4, 5, and 6 which varies according to the grade. I paid ¥15,000 (A$197, US$150) in Andy's sixth grade.

Financial assistance, subject to a means test, is also available to families who cannot afford educational expenses.

Are Foreigners Common?

It depends on the school and the area. Some areas attract large expatriate or guest-worker communities. Whereas expatriate families tend to choose international schools for their children, the guest workers generally gravitate toward the Japanese system. Our area was one with a high expatriate population of both business people and embassy personnel. In Andy's primary school there were two classes in each grade and, on average, one foreigner in each class. Several of the children were from the nearby French and Iranian embassies. There were also some Scandinavian, eastern European, Chinese, and Korean children. A number of Japanese children with one foreign parent were also attending.

Endnotes

1. See appendix for details of the form.
2. Japanese students at that time still attended school six days a week. In 1992, one Saturday a month became a rest day, and in 1995 a second was added.
3. Any foreigner is invited to attend the festival. Inquiries can be directed to the Chichibu City Office (tel: 0494-22-2211, 8:30–5:00 Monday to Friday, and 8:30–12:00 Saturday).
4. The rate of exchange which has been used throughout this text is ¥76 to the Australian dollar, ¥100 to the US dollar.
5. For the cost of the Japanese public system, see Appendix.
6. One tatami mat measures 6 feet by 3 feet (2 meters by 1 meter).
7. A futon is a Japanese bed which consists of a padded mattress over which you spread sheets and a quilt. All components fold up into a reasonably small space and are stored in a cupboard during the day.
8. A *hanko* is usually circular, about 2 centimeters in diameter, and gives the person's name in Chinese characters. Names of foreigners are usually written in the *katakana* script, but my *hanko* had been designed using Chinese characters, phonetically chosen to reflect my interest in intercultural communication.

9. Karen Hill Anton is an African-American woman who has lived with her family in Shizuoka prefecture for many years. She writes a regular column for *The Japan Times*, and has recently published a book about her experiences entitled *Crossing Cultures* (The Japan Times, 1993). The column quoted from was published in the October 22, 1992 edition of the paper.

10. *Jan ken poi* is the Japanese version of the game "rock, paper, scissors." However, in Japan it is used frequently by all age groups to determine turn-taking order, and its outcome is never questioned.

11. Under the numerous expressways running through the center of Tokyo, sports practice areas, parks, and parking lots have been built, where they are protected from the weather.

12. Quoted from "Preparing for the Twenty-first Century" in *The Future Image of Sophia University: Looking Towards the Twenty-first Century*. Ed. Mutsuo, Yanase, S.J. Tokyo: Sophia University Press, 1989. (p. 77)

Further Reading

For those interested in further reading on the subject of Japanese education and/or expectations for working in a Japanese company, a large number of works are available. Among them I would suggest the following:

For experiences in junior high school, *Learning to Bow* by Bruce S. Feiler (New York: Ticknor & Fields, 1991) is a delightful and very humorous book.

For more academic books on education, I would recommend *The Japanese Educational Challenge* by Merry White (Free Press, 1987) and *Japan's High Schools* by Thomas Rohlen (University of California Press, 1983).

In looking particularly at the relationship between culture and education, *Transcending Stereotypes*, edited by Barbara Finkelstein, Anne E. Imamura, and Joseph J. Tobin (Intercultural Press, 1991), makes very interesting reading.

Two very readable texts about working in the Japanese corporate environment are *On Track With the Japanese* by Patricia Gercik (Kodansha International, 1992) and *Working For a Japanese Company*, by Robert March (Kodansha International, 1992).

THE ANATOMY OF DEPENDENCE
Takeo Doi, M.D.
Translated by John Bester

A definitive analysis of *amae*, the indulging, passive love which supports an individual within a group, a key concept in Japanese psychology.

PB, ISBN 0-87011-494-8, 184 pages

THE ANATOMY OF SELF
The Individual Versus Society

Takeo Doi, M.D.
Translated by Mark A. Harbison

A fascinating exploration into the role of the individual in Japan, and Japanese concepts of self-awareness, communication, and relationships.

PB, ISBN 0-87011-902-8, 176 pages

BEYOND NATIONAL BORDERS
Kenichi Ohmae

"[Ohmae is] Japan's only management guru." — *Financial Times*

PB, ISBN 4-7700-1385-X , 144 pages
Available only in Japan.

THE BOOK OF TEA
Kakuzo Okakura
Foreword and Afterword by Soshitsu Sen XV

The seminal text on the meaning and practice of tea, illustrated with eight historic photographs.

PB, ISBN 4-7700-1542-9, 160 pages

THE COMPACT CULTURE
The Japanese Tradition of "Smaller is Better"

O-Young Lee
Translated by Robert N. Huey

A provocative study of Japan's tendency to make the most out of miniaturization, that reveals the essence of Japanese character.

PB, ISBN 4-7700-1543-3, 196 pages

DISCOVER JAPAN   Words, Customs, and Concepts
Volumes 1 & 2
The Japanese Culture Institute

Essays and photographs illuminate 200 ideas and customs of contemporary Japan. "The one book you must have if you're heading for Japan ..."   — *Essex Journal*

PB, Vol. 1: ISBN 0-87011-835-8, 216 pages
PB, Vol. 2: ISBN 0-87011-836-6, 224 pages

GEISHA, GANGSTER, NEIGHBOR, NUN
Scenes from Japanese Lives
Donald Richie

A collection of 48 highly personal portraits of Japanese—both famous and obscure. "His portraits are unforgettable."   — Tom Wolfe

PB, ISBN 4-7700-1526-7, 212 pages
Previously published in hardcover as Different People.

HAGAKURE
The Book of the Samurai
Tsunetomo Yamamoto
Translated by William Scott Wilson

"A guidebook and inspiration for ... anyone interested in achieving a courageous and transcendent understanding of life."   — *East West Journal*

PB, ISBN 0-87011-606-1, 180 pages

THE HIDDEN ORDER
Tokyo Through the Twentieth Century
Yoshinobu Ashihara
Translated by Lynne E. Riggs

Looking at architecture as a metaphor for culture, a renowned Japanese architect considers the apparent chaos of Tokyo.

PB, ISBN 4-7700-1664-6, 160 pages

THE JAPANESE EDUCATIONAL CHALLENGE
A Commitment to Children
Merry White

Examines educational values in Japan, and differences between the Japanese and American school systems. "The best account I know of Japan as a learning society."   — Ronald P. Dore

PB, ISBN 4-7700-1373-6, 224 pages
Available only in Japan.

THE JAPANESE NEGOTIATOR
Subtlety and Strategy Beyond Western Logic
Robert M. March

Shows how Japanese negotiate among themselves and examines case studies, providing practical advice for the Western executive.

PB, ISBN 0-87011-962-1, 200 pages

THE JAPANESE THROUGH AMERICAN EYES
Sheila K. Johnson

A revealing look at the images and stereotypes of Japanese produced by American popular culture and media.

PB, ISBN 4-7700-1450-3, 208 pages   Available only in Japan.

JAPAN'S LONGEST DAY
Pacific War Research Society

A detailed account of the day before Japan surrendered, based on eyewitness testimony of the men involved in the decision to surrender.

PB: ISBN 0-87011-422-0, 340 pages

MANGA! MANGA!
The World of Japanese Comics
Frederick L. Schodt
Introduction by Osamu Tezuka

A profusely illustrated and detailed exploration of the world of Japanese comics.

PB, ISBN 0-87011-752-1, 260 pages

NEIGHBORHOOD TOKYO
Theodore C. Bestor

A highly readable glimpse into the everyday lives, commerce, and relationships of some 2,000 neighborhood residents of Tokyo.

PB, ISBN 4-7700-1496-1, 368 pages   Available only in Japan.

THE INLAND SEA
Donald Richie

An award-winning documentary—part travelogue, part intimate diary and meditation—of a journey into the heart of traditional Japan.

PB, ISBN 4-7700-1751, 292 pages

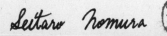